The Garden of Happiness

The Garden
Of
Happiness

Cultivating
True and Lasting Happiness
in Life

by

Kenneth N. Myers

Mayeux Press
SHERMAN, TEXAS

The Garden of Happiness
Cultivating True and Lasting Happiness in Life

© Copyright 2008 by Kenneth N. Myers

Unless otherwise indicated, Scripture is taken from the
HOLY BIBLE, NEW INTERNATIONAL VERSION.
Copyright 1973, 1978, 1984 International Bible Society
Used by permission of Zondervan Bible Publishers.

Myers, Kenneth Neal, 1959-
The Garden of Happiness: Cultivating True and Lasting Happiness
in Life/Kenneth N. Myers

ISBN 978-0-615-21762-8

1. Christian Living   2. Theology

248

Cover design: Neal Mayeux
Artwork: *An Italian Garden* by William Merritt Chase, 1909

Published by Mayeux Press
P.O. Box 3497, Sherman, TX 75091

To
Jerry and Patsy Hesley
for Sharing the Garden of their Happiness

Gerald and Colleen Frimann
whose Garden at the Cathedral brings Happiness to Many

In Loving Memory of Deidre Hopson
May her Heavenly Garden be Filled with Joy

Acknowledgements

Thank you to the good people of Christ Church Cathedral and the Diocese of the South Central who have encouraged and supported me these many years, and who have urged me to take up the pen and write.

Thank you to Carolyn Doby and Scott Rudy for their editing, proofreading, suggestions and insights.

Thank you to my wife, Shirley, for standing beside me all these years and supporting me in everything I have done. You make our Garden of Happiness a beautiful place.

All men know that the true good is Happiness, and all
men seek it, but, for the most part, by wrong routes -
like a drunk man who knows he has a house but can't
find his way home.
-C.S. Lewis, paraphrasing Boethius

Why, it's a happy road
That I'm travelin' on,
I just can't help myself,
You got me singin' a happy song.
-                        Barry McGuire

Table of Contents

Introduction

Serendipity Strikes Again

Serenity's a long time coming for me,
In fact I don't believe that I know what it means.
-John Denver

I am so tired of sourpuss Christians. The problem is not that they aren't much fun to be around (although I bet you would agree with me that they aren't). The problem is that sourpuss Christians have distorted the biblical portrayal of what true spirituality is all about.

Sourpuss Christians act like the more spiritual people become, the more somber and joy-killing they also become. They don't have time for fun. They wouldn't dare enjoy life - that would be "fleshly". Why, they are much too spiritual to laugh or play or show any signs of happiness. They don't have happiness, they tell us (and they erroneously tell us happiness is a surface thing that depends on what "happens"); instead they tell us they have "joy". They think joy is supposed to be some kind of deep, spiritual, interior quality that never

11

actually makes its way to the surface of their skin and never shows itself as a smile across the lips or a twinkle in the eyes. They insist they are full of joy, but not happiness, and that their joy is so deep as to be hidden.

I don't like them, and I bet you don't either. Unless you're one of them. And if you are one of them, chances are you still don't really like them, and you don't even like yourself.

Standing over against sourpuss Christians is the clear word of Scripture: "Happy is that people whose God is the Lord"[1] (and that's quoting from the good old King James Version, for those who are concerned that modern translators have botched things up by trading the word "blessed" for the word "happy"). If the Lord (Yahweh) is our God, then we ought to be a happy people. In fact, we have a responsibility to be a happy people!

There is a spiritual happiness that comes from being blessed by God that *ought* to be the native environment of God's people. It isn't some kind of "I'm spiritually happy, you just can't tell it" thing. True happiness is the kind of thing that affects us physically, socially, emotionally (what I mean is, incarnationally) - in other words, it affects our very countenance - when God lifts up his countenance upon us it gives us peace (so says

---

[1] Psalm 144.15

the blessing of Aaron[2]). But happiness is also a spiritual discipline - one sadly overlooked by many holier-than-thou people who think happiness is a sign of a lack of spirituality and that a truly godly spirituality will be shown by somberness and sobriety.

True happiness and true joy are virtually indistinguishable. While *any* blessing of God can become an idol, it is not the blessing that is the enemy, it is how we respond to the blessing. Happiness is a gift from God, literally. It is "blessedness". One *cannot* have joy without having happiness and vice versa. There are too many sourpusses walking around in the name of Jesus and all that is holy looking down judgmental noses at folk who are simply happy in the Lord and living lives of happiness, when the truth of the matter is those simple happy people are demonstrating the touch of God in

There are too many sourpusses walking around in the name of Jesus looking down judgmental noses at folk who are simply happy.

---

[2] Number 6.22ff

their lives much more than the spiritually elite in their pious religiosity.

"Happy is the man who walks not in the counsel of the ungodly, nor stands in the way of the sinner, nor sits in the seat of the scornful. He delights in the law and meditates on it day and night".[3]

This book began as a Lenten study, and I am sad to say that sourpuss Christians have practically kidnapped and held hostage the Church's season of Lent. Lent, we are told, should be forty days of back-whipping, introspection and self-condemnation. During these forty days we are directed (although no one would admit it) to pretend that Jesus had never died and risen from the grave, that he had never reconciled us to God, and that we are still lost in our sins. Lent, of course, is not about this at all, and those who go into the Lenten season every year with gray faces and blackened hearts miss the whole point of the season. Lent is not a time for condemnation and "woe is me". It is, instead, a time of rejoicing and celebrating that Christ has freed us from our sins and liberated us as sons and daughters of God. Lent is about us shucking off the things that keep us from true happiness. In the Eastern Church this season is referred to as "Happy Lent".

---

[3] Psalm 1.1

14

Interestingly, the actual word "Lent" isn't a religious term at all. It simply means "spring" - the time of year following winter when people plant their gardens. In this book we are going to approach the subject of happiness under the figure of a garden. We will discover that gardens aren't natural. They don't just happen. They take work, cultivation and care.

Coincidentally, a curiosity: late one Tuesday night (actually, early one Wednesday morning), as I was preparing to write this book, I was awaiting the "magic hour" between one and two a.m. when airlines discount their fares. I was whiling away the time reading a review[4] about a book entitled *Mapping Paradise*, showing what the ancients and the medievals thought about where the Garden of Eden was located.

Until very recent times (say, within the last three or four centuries) maps were designed with the east at the top, the west at the bottom, the north on the left and the south on the right. Ancient and medieval maps were a 90 degree turn from our maps, and we would get confused looking at them unless we understood this important difference. East was the primary direction, just as north is the primary direction for us today. While we might be tempted to consider those old maps and mapmakers to be "odd", it might just as likely be that *we*

---

[4] *In Search of Eden*, by Alan Jacobs, published in First Things, February 2007. Jacobs reviews *Mapping Paradise: A History of Heaven on Earth* by Alessandro Scafi, University of Chicago Press.

are the odd ones, for in the grand scheme of things (cosmically speaking) our north is no more "up" than their east. Pan out your camera from the earth, to the solar system, to the Milky Way and further, and you will discover that our idea of "up" (which we call north on a modern map) is a relative thing. The ancient way of mapmaking has at least one vestige that remains with us today. When we are on the road or a trail and pull out a map to find ourselves, and situate the map so that the map's north is facing our north, we call it "orienting" - "Just a moment here, and let me get oriented". But oriented, of course, means getting our bearings in regard to the Orient - the East. So although our primary direction is north, we still get "easted" or oriented. The word endures.

Now, where were we? Oh, yes - the ancients had their maps with the East on top, and the place that was - as Genesis tells us, "in the east"[5] - was the Garden of Eden. So the old maps show the Garden of Eden at the *top* of the world, and everything else below it. Thus, the old maps were not unlike a genealogical or chronological chart that would have Adam and Eve at the *top* and everyone else below them. We must at least hand it to our medieval ancestors for being consistent;

---

[5] Genesis 2.8

their system[6] had a pattern to it that our modern ones lack - geography and linear history "looked" the same: the beginning - time *and* place - on the top, everything else flowing down from that.

Back to the coincidental curiosity. In the book review I learned that some folk used to think the Garden of Eden was in what is now Sri Lanka, previously called Ceylon, and before that called (by the Romans) Serendip. *"Whaaaattt???"* - I'd never heard of Sri Lanka being called Serendip. I dug deeper into the matter (including visiting the official Sri Lankan website)[7] and learned that "dip" is an Indian (Pali) suffix for "island", and that "Seren" or "Sarana" (the original source of "serene") is Pali for "sanctuary". Sri Lanka's old name, Serendip, means "Island Sanctuary"; thus many believed it had been the *original* sanctuary - the Garden of Eden.

An old Persian tale, "The Three Princes of Serendip", about three princes from Sri Lanka who kept having good things befall them no matter what they faced, made it's way into Europe sometime before the

---

[6] For an enlightening and enjoyable survey of the Medieval Model for Everything, see C.S. Lewis' *The Discarded Image: An Introduction to Medieval and Renaissance Literature*, Cambridge, Cambridge University Press, 1964.

[7] http://www.news.lk/index.php? option=com_content&task=view&id=1420&Itemid=52

18th century and became a favorite of one Horace Walpole, who in 1754 coined the term "serendipity" to describe when good things happen in unexpected ways.

Serendipity - the befalling of good fortune in unexpected ways - but the word gets us back to the Garden, "the Island Sanctuary" - the enclosure of peace. So it was something of a coincidence, a serendipitous moment, when, as I began to write this book on the Garden of Happiness, that I happened upon Serendip and her three princes. As I said at the first, this is but a mere curiosity, and yet it was joyful for me, a lover of words.

Of course, no one knows where the Garden of Eden was (though many a huckster has tried to make a dishonest buck by proving it to be here or there), and even if we did know, and even if it were still there, we couldn't get in again, and even if we could, we couldn't long endure. There is, however, still a garden to be had, a Garden of Happiness, and it is given to us all to plant, cultivate and keep just such a garden in our own lives. Happiness doesn't come naturally. Happiness doesn't just happen, but God's Word and common sense give us the means to turn the howling wilderness into a Serene Sanctuary where God is King and Happiness rules the day.

I invite you to put on your gardening gloves, pull out your spade and rake, get your seeds and sprouts ready, and join with me as together we build the Garden of Happiness.

Chapter One

The Art of Gardening

You can't go home again. - Thomas Wolfe

Our story (and by that I mean *our* story - everyone's story) begins in a garden. Genesis 2.8 tells us, "The Lord God planted a garden toward the east, in Eden, and there he placed the man whom he had formed". Verse 15 continues, "Then the Lord God took the man and put him in the garden of Eden to cultivate it and to keep it."

Of course, you know the rest of the story, how Adam and Eve opted for Law (the tree of the *knowledge of good and evil*) over relationship (the tree of life) and traded their place in the garden for a little shack on the edge of the howling wilderness. Ever since that fateful day, humanity has been trying and failing to get back to the garden.[8] People have tried a million ways to reach back to that golden era, all to no avail. Yet there is something insatiable in the human appetite, something in our hearts that hearkens for Paradise - that yearns for a time and a place when all is well, where perfection is enjoyed, where our personal lives, our marriages, our friendships, our families, our jobs, our cities and our nations all enjoy a level of peace and serenity that is only momentarily glimpsed in our current condition.

You Can't Go Home Again

Can I give you some bad news? You can't go back. You can't go back to the Garden of Eden, you can't go back to the Golden Age, and you can't even go back to your own "good old days" which you remember with fondness.

Can I tell you some more bad news? Even if you could go back, you would be shocked and disappointed to discover that the past wasn't all it was cracked up to be.

---

[8] Genesis tells us that God appointed an angel with a flaming sword to guard the way back into the Garden. The Ancients believed that God actually removed the Garden completely and relocated it to the heavenly region ruled by Venus - the "third heaven." In 2 Corinthians 12.2ff, St. Paul mentions that he "knew a man" who was caught up into the "third heaven" - to "Paradise."

Ah, those golden days of yesteryear, when life was simpler and calmer and better. Every generation hearkens back to a golden era (it all started with Plato - more about that later), but of course, when it comes down to brass tacks, no one really thinks there was much gold back then.

I grew up in the sixties in rural north Texas. Those were my "golden days". The simplicity of life, the lack of stress, the freedom of childhood. Now, we didn't have air conditioning in our car, and on long trips to visit family in south Louisiana my father would buy blocks of ice and put them in a pan in the back floorboard of the car. We would roll down the windows and create a "water cooler" type of system that was a poor attempt to assuage the hot August sun and swampish humidity. I don't want to go back to *that* again. Recently my father had back surgery and was released, walking, the next day. I remember my grandfather having back surgery 40 years ago and having to lie completely still in a hospital bed for several weeks. I don't want to go back to *that* again. When it comes to doing research I can have a book delivered from an online bookseller to my door in two days or less. For goodness sake, I have Wikipedia and the internet and a whole world of

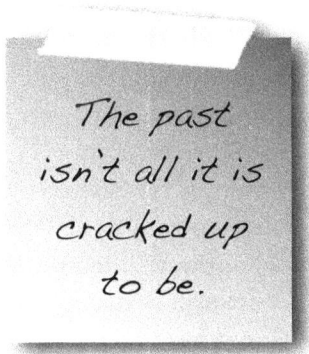

The past isn't all it is cracked up to be.

information at the tips of my fingers.[9] I remember being taken by my grandmother to get my own library card. She taught me to love books. When I was in school I used to go to the library to research things. It was a small town library with very limited research capabilities, and I couldn't find half the answers I looked for. I don't want to go back to *that* again.

My "good old days" are not worth comparing to my father's! He remembers with fondness his simpler days growing up a Cajun outdoorsman along the banks of the Missisippi River with a life akin to Tom Sawyer and Huckleberry Finn. Days spent hunting with his brothers, skipping school every Friday to help his father fish, and staying with relatives who lived in a houseboat on the river. However, those days also meant picking cotton in the blistering sun for days on end and mere coins as payment. Those days meant his whole family being flooded from their home, packing all they had into boats and floating downriver until they found a suitable spot where they disembarked, chopped down trees, and built another home. He doesn't want to go back to *that* again.

I'm sitting here writing this book on an Apple MacBook (I admit it, here is my shameless plug for the best computers money can buy). I can move text

---

[9] A fascinating book on how technology is changing not only small town America but the whole world is Thomas Friedman's *The World is Flat* (2005, Farrar, Strauss & Giroux).

around, delete, or go back to a previous section and add paragraphs. When I was in Bible School I used to go rent an electric typewriter for five dollars a day to type up my papers. If I made mistakes on a page I had to start all over. Before that I had to write on a manual typewriter, and before that I had to use pen and paper. My father tells of his school days when he was so poor he had to look around for little pencil scraps left on the school ground by other students. I don't want to go back to *that* again.

It All Started with Plato

Let me get philosophical with you for a page or two. I promise it won't hurt, and if I do my job well enough, and if you are patient enough with me, some good might come of this little rabbit trail.

The idea of a golden age began with the Greek philosopher Plato. In *The Republic*, Plato taught that change was a bad thing, because change was always moving *away* from those ancient, mythical golden days of perfection and *toward* imperfection. The idea was something like this: if the original of a thing was perfect, then every subsequent copy of it was less perfect. Copies of copies of copies led to modifications that led to poorer quality (to illustrate the idea, try playing the "telephone" game with a dozen people in a circle where you whisper a message to the one next to you and tell them to "pass it on", or copy a photo in a copying machine, then copy that copy and so on for about a dozen times). Thus, the fewer changes made - the fewer copies, the fewer modifications - the closer to the original a thing remained, and the closer to perfection. The mythical ancient days of Athens had been a perfect golden age. The emergence of new forms and structures of government and society threatened to significantly change things.

Plato really hated democracy. He was a totalitarian thinker and the father of future totalitarians like Stalin and Hitler. He hated democracy for a couple of reasons. One was his assumption that the new idea of democracy was a significant change from the ancient model of totalitarianism that had existed in Athens. Change, remember, is bad. Another reason he hated democracy was because it put people on a level playing field and gave actual individual freedom, and if people had freedom, and didn't stay in their predestined class roles - in other words, if choice was *decentralized* - why, all sorts of havoc would ensue and all sorts of change would come about, and that couldn't be good on any level!

Let me make a clarification: for Plato there was one, and only one, kind of change that was good: change that got us back toward that ideal, that perfect age. Of course, the definition of perfection was held and maintained only by the Philosopher King himself. Thus, if any change was made, it could only be made in the direction of "the ideal" by consent of the Philosopher

King. In other words, the King held the blueprint to what a perfect society and state looked like, and if *any* changes were going to be made, they were going to be made by the permission and direction of the King, and only as a means of getting to the ideal.

What this called for was centralized control, because change had to be controlled. Free change (and free exchange) could only lead to chaos and devolution and bad copies of bad copies that led to the worsening, not bettering, of things. If there was going to be change, it had to be toward the blueprint of perfection and it had to be centrally controlled and applied wholesale to everything and everyone. This, obviously, is the model embraced by all totalitarian despots, by Marxists, and particularly by the Soviet Union. The central authority has to control everything - for the sake of achieving the ideal - and so every aspect of life is under the control of the TOTALitarian government: business, education, religion, economics, philosophy, family, entertainment, communications and everything else you can list.

Little children growing up in totalitarian systems (whether Plato's Athens, Hitler's Germany, Castro's Cuba or, God-forbid, a future United States of America) are all taught the ideal to be achieved - "the 1000 years of the Third Reich", the "Fatherland of Russia" - the restoration of a greatness held in the past but lost in the present and to be recovered under the controlling hand of centralized authority. If, on the other hand, you grew up in a free society (say, the United States of the late twentieth century) you weren't taught about a past golden age, nor about a future golden age. There was no blueprint showing who and what we would look like 500 years down the road. A free society doesn't seek to control change or direct it toward a particular ideal, and in fact understands that the freedom to make changes is the engine that brings about creative improvements to all areas of life. Just compare automobiles from a totalitarian society (where centralized control determines *wholesale* change, if any at all) with the automobiles of a free society (where *piecemeal* change is encouraged and one company makes an improvement, copied by others, who then make further improvements themselves). Change can make things better and can alleviate suffering. Change can be good. Here is the important thing: there is no ideal past, and there is no blueprint for the future.[10]

OK. Now we're finished with the little philosophical excursion. Did you get it all? The point really is this: not only can we not go back to the "good old days" because of the sheer impossibility of retro time travel, not only can we not go back to the "good old days" because they really never were that good, we also cannot go forward to the "good old days" because there is no "ideal" in the future either. We can't go backward because of the

_____

[10] For a stunningly good book on this subject I recommend Sir Karl Popper's *The Open Society and Its Enemies, Volume One: Plato* (1971, Princeton Univeristy Press).

temporal impossibility, and we can't recreate a perfect time in the future because there is no blueprint to build on. According to the Bible, Paradise won't be restored until the end of history. Perfection will not come until He-Who-Is-Perfect comes. Any time a church or religious group gets the idea that they are going to bring about perfection before the Second Coming, the results are always catastrophic and destructive, whether that be David Koresh and the Branch Davidians or Ulrich Zwingli and the Anabaptists.[11]

> *There is no blueprint showing exactly what life will be like in the future. The future is ours to make.*

We want Paradise, but we're not going to get it this side of Christ's Return. So, what do we do in the meantime? We build a garden.

---

[11] I would suggest that any institution (family, civil, church, business, etc.) that insists on centralized control and the curbing of the freedom of change ought to be avoided, changed if possible, and fled if not. This is by no means an endorsement of anarchy, but a call for the recognition of the proper role of centralized authority - what Popper calls "quality control."

Gardens Are Artificial

Gardens are not natural. They are not found in nature. Walk up on a garden in the middle of a wilderness and the first conclusion you would come to is that "someone else has been here." Gardens are artificial. Gardens are the result of artifice - having to do with art. Artifice means a skillfully contrived work. Artificial doesn't mean "fake", it means "shaped".

Maybe you remember that old story about the man who labored for years to produce a beautiful garden only to have a stranger pass by and say, "Oh my, what a beautiful thing God has created." To which the man replied, "Yes, but you should have seen this place when God had it to himself." The Bible tells us that God created a garden in the east, and he placed man in that garden to *work* it and to *care* for it. As any gardener knows, left to itself even the loveliest of gardens will soon revert to the wilds of nature.

You need to know that nature is not all it is cracked up to be. I was just a young teenager at the tail-end of the hippie movement, but I remember all the talk about "back to nature". I loved John Denver's *Rocky Mountain High*, and I liked John Lennon's *Mother Nature's Son*, but John Denver never really lived out in nature, and John Lennon wouldn't have known what to do if he'd found himself dealing face to face with Mother Nature. Nature is scary.

When each of my three children graduated from High School, I told them I would take them anywhere in the world they wanted to go (at that time I was traveling a lot and had accumulated many frequent flyer miles so I could fly for free). My daughter chose Paris. My eldest son chose Spain. My youngest son walked in one day, slapped me on the back, and said, "Dad, we're going to the Galapagos." I didn't even know where the Galapagos Islands were! I had to look them up on a map and discovered that they were six hundred miles west of Quito, Ecuador. Famous as the scene of Charles Darwin's excursions on the *HMS Beagle*, and noted as an almost Edenic archipelago where the animals were "tame", we spent five days on a boat moving from island to island, seeing an amazing array of animals that, in any other context, would have scurried away at first sight, but in the Galapagos were docile enough to become a nuisance blocking every pathway. We had to tiptoe through fields of huge iguanas, shoo crabs away from our feet, and gently avoid stepping on unmoving and unmovable Blue-footed Boobies. Sitting on the beach, my son actually had a bird land on his foot! Our first day there we jumped into the water for a swim, only to be greeted by playful sea lions. "Sea lions!", we exclaimed in joy. By our last day we were saying, "Sea lions" - not in joy, but in perturbance.

The Galapagos experience was an anomaly. The next week we flew from Quito into the Amazon Basin to

31

the frontier town of Coco. Coco was a scary place. The main street going through the middle of town was rough and seemed to be filled not with crushed gravel but with football sized rocks. Every inch of riding in the back of a truck meant being bounced what seemed like three feet high. All along the way the locals looked at us like we had no business being there. After sitting a couple of hours awaiting our next mode of transportation, we boarded a small boat powered by an outboard motor and rode downriver, 120 miles from the nearest electricity. Now we were in the middle of the Amazon Jungle. For the next five days our home was a bamboo hut, and we were guided through the jungle by two guides - an Indian who spoke the native dialect and Spanish, and who had lived his whole life in the jungle, and a young man from Quito who spoke English and Spanish. The Indian guide would communicate to the other guide who would communicate to us. We were cautioned about poisonous snakes. We were warned about quicksand. We were told of vampire bats. We were warned not to stray from camp at night - jaguars were creatures of the night, after all. Ah, nature! Rats the size of raccoons sneaking into our room at night to

Nature is a dangerous place. There are things in nature that will eat you!

get to our snack food. Ah, nature! We had to sleep with mosquito nets to keep out not only the mosquitoes but also the foot-long centipedes and painful scorpions. Ah, nature! Mercy, even the *fish* in the Amazon will eat you! Aaargh, nature!

Does anyone here remember the Fall? Nature isn't all sweet and beautiful and perfect! It's a howling wilderness. It's a killer. It is beautiful from a distance, or for a day, or from the safety of modern conveniences - there's nothing quite like driving in a comfortable air-conditioned car through the scenic mountains of North Carolina. But try it 400 years ago, when there were things that could eat you before you could eat them. Or try it now - dropped into the middle of some mountain range - with no knife, no gun, no compass, no fishing equipment, no extra clothing (no, let's be natural here - how about no clothing at all?), no cell phone, no first aid kit and no matches. Just you and nature. Lovely idea, isn't it?

Gardens are not natural. They are artistic creations out of nature. I remember another trip I took, for a meeting of bishops in Great Britain. On a free day we toured a castle which, although a tourist attraction, was still the home of an aristocratic family. The building and the furniture were impressive, but what really attracted everyone - what demanded the focus of our eyes, the meandering of our feet and the time we had on hand - was the garden. Beautifully sculpted hedges surrounded flowers of every kind and color. Fountains sprayed up here and there. Rows of carefully crafted trees lined footpaths from one place to another. Benches were situated in perfect spots to sit and consider the beauty of the surroundings. *Someone* was an artist! While we were there we noticed men in various parts of the garden doing hedge work or watering the plants - this thing didn't just spring up on its own!

Gardens are not natural, but nature is the medium with which a gardener works to bring about the creation of a skillfully designed work of art.

Happiness Isn't Natural

Have you ever heard someone excuse some flaw in their character by saying, "That's just the way I am," or (in a more blame-shifting response), "That's just the way the Good Lord made me"? Have you ever had someone haul off and smack you with hurtful words, and then later say, "Oh, I'm sorry, but that's just my human nature"? Human nature is a lot like Amazon nature. Left to itself it is deadly.

In the midst of a wilderness, God called the first pair of humans to be gardeners, and he has called all of their sons and daughters to be the same. He invites us to join with him in creating works of beauty. He provides the raw stuff of nature - whether that be a plot of ground to be tilled or a human soul to be cultivated - and he asks us to work with what he has given us and make something good and beautiful with it.

One of the first mistakes people make about happiness is they assume that happiness is their natural state. It isn't. The natural state of fallen man is despair. That Christ has come and brought about the beginning of a New Creation makes us people of hope - we have something to look forward to and something to work toward; but happiness doesn't just happen. Nor is happiness rooted in what happens to us or around us. True, godly happiness is the result of an interior gardening experience. We have to go into our inner being, pull up the briars and brambles, clear out the ground of our heart, plant good plants, fertilize the ground, water the plants, weed out the weeds, place a gazebo over here and a sitting bench over there, an ornament in that corner and a fountain just so. Happiness comes as we cultivate the Garden of God in our own lives.

The Bible begins with a garden and ends with a city - the Bride of Christ. However, the city described in the last chapters of Revelation is not a drab city full of filth and crime and congestion. Nor is an overcrowded city full of buildings that look like concrete mountains with people living inside them. It is, rather, a city beautifully "adorned"[12] - dressed up, cultivated, arranged - things

---

[12] Revelation 21.2

placed upon her to make her gorgeous - not naturally, but artfully made. And in the middle of the city is a garden! And the garden is filled with trees that are trees of life, each bearing fruit in season, and whose leaves are for the healing of the nations.[13] The fullness of that city will not be seen until the Day of the Lord, but that garden, that heavenly city, *begins now*, and the first step toward experiencing it is to understand that godly happiness takes work. As a result of the Fall, Adam was cursed to work by the sweat of his brow, but I believe before the fall, when he was a gardener in Eden, he whistled while he worked. When you are blessed of the Lord you whistle while you work, because you are busy about the business of building for Paradise.

In the next chapter we will learn together about the fundamental law of gardening: whether we're raising a crop of tomatoes or a crop of happiness, we reap what we sow.

---

[13] Revelation 22.2

Chapter Two

You Reap What You Sow

"Just a little old fashioned karma coming down.
A little old fashioned justice going round.
A little bit of sowing and a little bit of reaping,
A little bit of laughing and a little bit of weeping.
Just a little old fashioned karma coming down."
-
                                        -Willie Nelson

God wants his people to be happy. I could say that
in other words: "God wants his people to be joyful," but
as soon as I said it, someone would go off and get all
spiritual on me and dissociate joy from happiness. I had
a priest write me once asking me if I didn't think that
happiness could actually be the enemy of true joy. I
responded with a simple response: "No!" Joy and
happiness are synonymous in Scripture, as is the word
blessed. Don't believe it when super-spiritual Christians
tell you that they are joyful but not happy. It isn't

possible. "*Happy* is that people whose God is the Lord," the Psalmist sang.[1]

Let me make it clear that what we're talking about here is godly happiness. Worldly happiness is superficial and depends on the moment. It depends on what is happening in life today. Godly happiness is deep and it is rooted in the things of God. This kind of happiness can be attained even in the midst of trials and difficulties. The Hebrew word for "blessed" literally means "multiple happinesses". When Jesus said, "Blessed are those who hunger and thirst after righteousness," he was saying, "Granted a multitude of happinesses are those who hunger and thirst after righteousness."

Blessed literally means " multiple happinesses." And God wants to bless you!

The Law of Reciprocity

Saint Paul, writing to the Christians in Galatia, told them, "Do not be deceived: God is not mocked, for whatever one sows, that will he also reap."[2] This is called the Law of Reciprocity, and Paul wasn't the first

---

[1] Psalm 144.15, KJV

[2] Galatians 6.7

one to come up with it. It is in the Old Testament, it is in the teachings of Jesus, it is in the sacred text of other world religions. The Buddhists call it Karma (although their understanding involves reaping in a reincarnated life). Old timers say, "What goes around comes around" and "If you want to dance, you have to pay the fiddler." Our actions have consequences. We reap what we sow.

Since Paul himself used a gardening analogy it works well with our theme. Have you ever sown a seed in the ground of your garden, thinking it was one thing, and finding out later that it was something else? I have planted what I thought was squash only to find out it was cucumber. But you can't plant corn and expect it to come up watermelon. You can't plant beans and expect to get peppers. In the Garden of our Life the principle is the same - whatever we plant in that garden, that's the fruit we're going to harvest.

Now, it would be a foolish thing to even have a garden at all if we reaped on a 100% basis. In other words, if I planted one kernel of corn in order to reap one kernel of corn, I may as well avoid the hassle and just stick with the first kernel I had. Why go to all the labor, the nurture, the watering and weeding, just to get back exactly what I put in the ground to begin with? In the Parable of the Talents[3] Jesus told of three men who were given money by their master and were directed to

---

[3] Matthew 25.14-30

put it to good use until he returned. When he returned much later one of the men had doubled the money from ten talents to twenty talents. Another had doubled it from five talents to ten; but the third, fearful of the master, had taken his money and hidden it away. He brought it to the master and said, "Look! I kept it safe for you! I'm giving back exactly what you gave me." The master, to say the least, was not a happy camper. He said, "You could have at least put it in a savings account and drawn a little interest! Yet because you did nothing with it, I'm taking it away from you and giving it to someone who will be fruitful with it." Then he kicked the servant out of his villa and onto the street, poorer but hopefully wiser. The laws of nature, and of the Kingdom of God, teach us that when we sow something we reap more of the same. If we sow one kernel of corn, we will reap hundreds of kernels. If we sow one watermelon seed, we will reap many watermelons and thousands of seeds! Now, here is the scary thing: it works the same way in the Garden that is our life: if we sow a little bit of hatred, we will reap much hatred. If we sow a little bit of condemnation, we will reap much condemnation. One seed of ill-speaking will reap a bushel of ill-speaking. The obverse is also true. A little kindness sown into the lives of others will reap for us a bounty of kindness. Just a cup of water, given in Jesus name, will bring great reward, Jesus' tells us.[4]

---

[4] Matthew 10.42

Some people - Christians, mind you - assume that because they are saved by the grace of God and God is not counting their sins against them,[5] they can live in any wicked way they choose without it having repercussions either in the here or the hereafter. However, the book of Job says, "Those who plow iniquity and sow trouble reap the same."[6] Whether a person is a Christian or not, whether they are saved by grace or not, the rule of reciprocity still applies.

Have you ever known people that had a mean streak to them, and no matter what situation they walked into they left it in tumult and chaos? I once knew a Christian man who was a "worthless person." I am not judging him, I am just quoting Scripture! Proverbs tells us, "A worthless person, a wicked man, goes about with crooked speech, winks with his eyes, signals with his feet, points with his finger, with perverted heart devises evil, continually sowing discord."[7] Did you notice the reference to gardening? This worthless person, Proverbs says, is "continually sowing discord." What do you think this person is going to reap? Why, discord by the bushel barrel, of course! This fellow had crooked speech - he would say one thing to one person and the

---

[5] Ephesians 2.8ff, 2 Corinthians 5.19

[6] Job 4.8

[7] Proverbs 6.12

opposite to the other, unconcerned for truth and integrity. He winked with his eyes, signaled with his feet and pointed with his finger - that is, he connived. He worked a situation dishonestly for his own advancement. He continually sowed discord - he couldn't be in any given situation very long before there was trouble stirred up, and it always pointed back to him. Most of the time he seemed to disentangle himself

> One of the reasons I am quick to show mercy, is because I know how much mercy I need. My motives are less than pure!

from it and shift the blame to someone else, but in the end it caught up with him. It began with people not wanting to be around him much. It continued with people starting to see through his scheming. Eventually no one trusted him or believed what he said. In the end his whole world fell apart and he found himself a bitter and lonely man alienated from fellow Christians, having reaped a cartload of what he had sown.

Speaking through the prophet Ezekiel God says, "According to their way I will do to them, and according to their own judgments I will judge them; and they shall

know that I am the Lord."[8] One of the reasons that I try
to be quick to show mercy to others, is because I know
that I myself am in great need of mercy from God and
from others! I will admit to you right now that my
motives are less than pure, and that I do this in an
attempt to save my own skin. Jesus said, "Blessed are
the merciful, for they shall obtain mercy."[9] He said, "Do
not judge, and you will not be judged."[10] I understand
that I am going to reap a compounded harvest of what I
sow, and, "According to my way he will do to me." Do
you remember the parable that Jesus told about the
Unmerciful Servant?[11] A man owed his boss something
like $250,000. When the time came to pay up, he didn't
have the money and begged mercy from his boss. The
boss didn't just give him an extension of time to come up
with the money, he completely cancelled the debt. "You
don't owe me a dime." Thrilled silly, the man walks out
of the office and onto the street, and in a cocky mood
sees a fellow worker that owes him $20. He goes over
and grabs the poor guy by his collar and says, "Pay up,
right now!" Of course, word got back to the boss and he
reeled the great debtor back into his office and said,
"You scumbag! I forgave you a great debt, and you can't
forgive your brother a small one?" Then he had the

---

[8] Ezekiel 7.27

[9] Matthew 5.7

[10] Luke 6.37

[11] Matthew 18.21-35

43

fellow thrown into debtors' prison until every penny of the debt could be paid! I, for one, know that I have been forgiven a great debt, and so I make it a point to show as much mercy as I possibly can. I know I'm going to reap what I sow.

We are all going to reap, in spades, what we have sown. It would be wise of us, then, to sow good seed. The prophet Hosea wrote[12], "Sow for yourselves righteousness; reap steadfast love." The Hebrew word for "steadfast love" is *hesed* - lovingkindness; mercy. Hosea continues, "Break up your fallow ground, for it is the time to seek the Lord, that he may come and rain righteousness upon you."

Friend, you and I both need the righteousness of God rained down on us. Our own righteousness is like "filthy rags" the Bible tells us. If we are going to have the fruit - the bounty - of righteousness in our lives, it needs to be rained down on us from God. When we break up the hard ground of our hearts, through humility and forgiveness, and when we sow a little righteousness, God will send his rains upon us and we will harvest a bumper crop, not of our own goodness, but of the goodness of God in our lives.

As I mentioned before, some people assume that because they are saved by grace, then it doesn't *matter*

---

[12] Hosea 10.12

what they think, say or do in life. Their assumptions seem to run on the channel that all our works are of no consequence in the New Covenant of Christ. But just take a read-through of the New Testament, from Jesus to John, from Matthew to Revelation, and notice just how important our works are, and how they *matter* in this life and the next! Not only are we told that we will reap what we sow, we are told that we will give an account for what we have done in the body[13], and that indeed we were born again *in order to* do good works![14]

Does the grace of God have no effect then? Of course it does! First, the grace of God supplies the energy for us to live a life sowing good things. Second, grace completely frees us from the eternal condemnation and the estrangement from God that might come from the bad things we have sown. Finally, *sometimes* in the economy of God, grace even frees us from reaping the fruit of the bad seeds we have sown. When someone sows bad fruit, earnestly repents and turns to God, seeks amendment of life and begins sowing good seed, oftentimes God's grace is at work chopping down the evil plants and weeds we have sown before they can bear bad fruit. One of my favorite U2 songs is *Grace*[15] -"Grace, it's the name of a girl, it's also a thought that

---

[13] 2 Corinthians 5.10

[14] Ephesians 2.10

[15] *Grace*, from the U2 album *All That You Can't Leave Behind*, 2000.

can change the world." Bono goes on to sing (and here is the line I love), "She travels outside of Karma." Sometimes grace works in our lives so that we don't reap the bad that we sow, but sometimes grace allows us to reap it and taste the horrible flavor, so that we will turn from it and not sow that seed anymore.

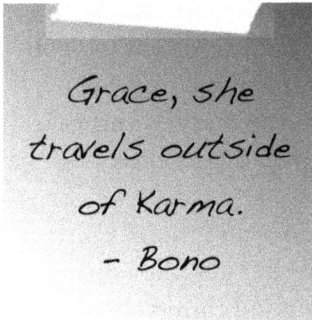

Grace, she travels outside of Karma.

- Bono

Sowing Happiness

Thomas Reeves is a retired professor of history, a Christian man, and a Roman Catholic. He is very smart, and he is the typical professor of history. Although a Christian, he was also, by his own admission, a cranky old man who thought himself smarter than most (a true thought) and considered it his intellectual responsibility to eschew happiness. As an older man, he admitted "throughout my rather long life I have never been attracted to cheery people..." In fact, he wrote, "I wanted to be the exact opposite, someone who was 'realistic', 'honest', and 'truthful'...I thought it appropriate to be serious to the point of being grave...I went a short step further, becoming something of a curmudgeon[16], [one whose] weapons are irony, satire, sarcasm, ridicule..."[17]

Have you ever known a curmudgeon? A grumpy old man or woman? Have you ever known people of any age who were critical and insulting and negative, who couldn't say anything good, but still said something? Have you noticed that after a while, even you with your own charming ways, just can't stand the pressure of their acidic tongue anymore? What happens then? You try to be nice, you try to be kind, you try to respond to their negativity with something positive, but eventually it happens - you dish out to them what they've been dishing out to you and others. They start reaping what they've sown, and suddenly, everywhere they go and everyone they encounter turns out to be reflecting that curmudgeon spirit right back onto them. It can be a dangerous downward spiral where they end up old and angry and alone, the whole world having rejected them because they rejected the whole world. They reap what they sow.

But I digress - Thomas Reeves, late in life, came to the realization that "this negative cast of mind discourages rather than helps others get through life in a healthy, happy, productive way, [and] it clashes strongly with the Christian faith, a religion of love and hope..."

---

[16] A bad tempered or surly person.

[17] *Mere Cheer*; Touchstone Magazine, December 2006

Here are his final words: "Cheerfulness, however forced, can generate both of these virtues."[18]

We have a responsibility to others to be cheerful and happy. "However forced," Dr. Reeves writes! Even if you are not particularly cheerful or happy, you have a Christian responsibility to cultivate these qualities and share them with others. The Twelve Step programs such as Alcoholics Anonymous have a maxim that is apropos: "Fake it 'til you make it." Even if it is not your inclination to show mercy or to be cheerful or to demonstrate kindness toward others - do it anyway! And keep doing it until it becomes true to who you are. No more talk about "it's not my nature" - your nature stinks! Your nature is fallen. Your nature is like your righteousness - filthy and corrupt! God is in the business of changing your nature and transforming you into his image. He has given Christ as both a *means* of that change ("the means of grace"[19]) and as a *model* of that change.

---

[18] Ibid.

[19] The wonderful Anglican prayer of General Thanksgiving says, "We thine unworthy servants do give Thee most humble and hearty thanks for all thy goodness and lovingkindness to us and to all men. We bless Thee for our creation, preservation and all the blessings of this life, but *above all for thine inestimable love in the redemption of the world by our Lord Jesus Christ, for the means of grace and for the hope of glory.*

You and I are going to reap what we sow. If we sow happiness into the lives of others, we are going to reap happiness in our own lives. None of us are going to encourage others, bless others, strengthen others, and send them on their way toward being better in life by being grumpy! However, if we sow goodness and cheer and happiness and encouragement and mercy into the lives of others, we will reap it ourselves, in multiplied returns.

What You Sow In Others You Reap In Yourself

How you treat others is how you are going to be treated. The Golden Rule (found, by the way, in all the world religions) instructs us "Do unto others as you would have others do unto you."[20] Jesus wasn't just whistling Dixie when he said this. It is a Kingdom principle and it is a law like the law of gravity. It is not a suggestion, it is not even a command. It is a commentary on how the universe works.

Jesus wasn't just whistling Dixie when he said, "Do unto others as you would have others do unto you."

---

[20] Matthew 7.12

Saint Josemaria Escriva (the founder of Opus Dei), said, "A piece of advice on which I have insisted repeatedly: be cheerful, always cheerful. It is for those to be sad who do not consider themselves to be sons of God...[Have] a sincere resolution: to make the way lovable for others and easy, since life brings enough bitterness with it already."[21]

One evening many years ago I was traveling through a large city late at night and I was thirsty. It was just a few minutes before 11 and I pulled into a fast food restaurant that was just about ready to close. I stood in line behind this obnoxious woman who was upset that her just-delivered hamburger didn't have a toasted bun. "I used to work in one of these stores," she said, "and I know the rules. You *have* to toast the bun if the customer wants it; and I want it."

The poor woman behind the counter was obviously exhausted, ready to go home and frustrated. "Look, I'll *give* you the hamburger, no charge. Will that work?"

"No! I want my hamburger and I want the bun toasted."

"But we've already turned off the toaster."

---

[21] *Furrow*, Josemaria Escriva de Balaguer, New York, Scepter Publishers, 2002; p. 28

"I don't care. Turn it back on."

The woman heated up the toaster, toasted the bun, gave the customer her burger and then looked at me and apologized for the scene.

"All I want is a medium Diet Coke," I said. Then, when I paid for my drink I tipped her twenty dollars. "You need to know that not all customers are jerks like that woman." I gave it to her in the name of Jesus and told her, "God bless you." It made her day. I was able to turn her evening around. I transformed it from a bad night to a good night. I didn't do it because I'm a saint. I did it because I know I'm going to reap what I sow.

Every person you meet this week is a field in which you can sow something. What they need from you (even the worst of them) is not condemnation or judgment or criticism or disdain. What they need from you is mercy and love and kindness and goodness and maybe a smile and a helping hand. Maybe they need a $5 tip for a $2 cup of coffee. Maybe they need a kind word.

God has given us this economy, this arrangement, that whatever it is we sow into the lives of others can be multiplied back into our own lives time and time again, pressed down, shaken together, and spilling out all over[22].

---

[22] Luke 6.38

In the next chapter, we will explore some of the "weeds" that might spring up in our garden and choke the good things planted there.

Chapter Three

"Ugly" Weeds

Happiness must be cultivated. It is like character.
It is not a thing to be safely let alone for a moment, or it
will run to weeds.
-Elizabeth Stuart Phelps

Bob Wills, the great Texas Troubadour and leader of
the Western Swing band *The Texas Playboys*, used to
"hawww" in between verses of his songs and throw out
funny little sayings. One of the funniest things he said
was, "Shoot low boys, they're riding Shetlands."

I am all for shooting high. I believe we should set
our sights for the stars. If we aim high we may miss our
mark, but if we aim low our mark probably is not worth
hitting. God has placed it in the heart of humanity to
achieve. St. Paul even tells us to "aim for perfection"[1].

---

[1] 2 Corinthians 13.11

May I introduce you to my friend, Reality? If you expect things to always go right and never go wrong, you are going to be sorely disappointed! There is a crude bumper sticker that you've probably seen so I won't repeat it here in exactly the same language, but the message is rock-solid true: poopoo happens!

Expect To Be Disappointed

I have a good friend who spent his life in the sales world. He is retired now and has a comfortable life. In fact, I'm writing this book from his house in North Carolina overlooking the Smoky Mountains. When I'm finished writing for the day my wife Shirley and I will take his little red convertible and ride into town for dinner. He and his wife are the picture of hospitality and generosity and they are just fun folk to be around. If you spent an evening with them I promise you would like them (and he might even let you take his car for a spin). If you spent an evening with them you would think they were the American Dream come true. They are not wealthy but they are comfortable. They enjoy life. God is good to them. They have some nice things. They have a great family, all serving God. What a charmed life! However, if you were to spend a few days with them instead of just an evening, and hear their whole story, you would be amazed that they have survived the curve balls life has thrown at them. More than once they have built up successful businesses only to have them unexpectedly taken away and find themselves left with nothing. They have endured family troubles in the past that if you heard the stories they would make your hair stand on end. They have both battled and beaten cancer. If they had gone through life expecting it to be perfect, with no problems or setbacks, they would have despaired and collapsed under the weight of the oppression, but they didn't expect perfection so they weren't devastated when troubles came. They endured. They survived. And in the end they thrived.

I have known other Christians who assumed that becoming a Christian meant a life of roses from here to hereafter. When bad times came they fell completely apart. I am a bishop in the Anglican tradition and one of the things I do is celebrate the Sacrament of Confirmation. It is a powerful sacrament and the Holy Spirit does some wonderful things in

First I anoint them with oil, then I slap them. Because following Jesus isn't all fun feelings and sweetness.

people's lives at this service. However, there is one little moment in the service that is very significant. First I anoint the confirmand with holy oil. Then I slap them! Now I will admit that some folk get slapped harder than other folk, but the slap is to remind them that following Jesus isn't all fun feelings and sweetness. Sometimes trouble comes from following Jesus. Sometimes Jesus' followers get rejected by others. Sometimes they get killed. His twelve closest friends, except John, all died horrible deaths, from being crucified upside down to being beheaded to being skinned alive! Jesus never promised them a rose garden. And if you think John was the lucky one, I should let you know that he was boiled alive in oil and miraculously delivered - oh, and that was after being exiled to a rock island off the coast of Asia Minor. It reminds me of what Saint Teresa of Avila said to God: "If this is the way you treat your friends, no wonder you have so few of them!"

Saint Teresa of Avila told God, "If this is the way you treat your friends, no wonder you have so few of them!"

One of the biggest setbacks in having a Garden of Happiness is expecting weeds not to grow. Trust me. They will grow, and you have to do some serious weeding work to keep them at bay.

Some of the weeds can't be avoided and just have to be plucked up when we see them. Some of the weeds

are our own doing and can be rooted out as soon as we
see the sprouts.

I Hate Entropy

I hate entropy. Entropy is a scientific term meaning
"a thermodynamic quantity representing the
unavailability of a system's thermal energy for
conversion into mechanical work, often interpreted as
the degree of disorder or randomness in the system."
Yes, I knew when you read the definition that you
would hate it too! Now let me tell you what it means, in
layman's terms: things fall apart. Things are always in
the process of decay. If you paint a house and come
back ten years later to check on it, the house will not be
better painted, it will be cracked and peeling. Entropy. If
you stack wood into a beautiful stack and come back six
months later to see it, it will not be *better* stacked, it will
be falling apart. The natural state of things is to go from
array to disarray (Ah! Nature!).

Entropy happens in our spiritual gardens too! I have
a friend who sometimes misses regular worship with
God's people for a while and wonders why her spiritual
life gets into a mess. Hmmmm...Let me see...go for a
month or two without being fed the Word of God, being
fed the Presence of Christ in the Sacraments, praising
God in worship, fellowshipping with God's people - I
wonder why her spiritual life starts to drift? One of the
dangers Christians face is the idea that we can bottle up

our spiritual life, cork it, and it will stay full. Have you figured out yet that your bottle leaks? It has cracks in it and it has to be kept full. Entropy is as true of spiritual things as it is of physical things. This is why it is deadly to think, "If I could just achieve *this, then* I would be happy." We can never "arrive" this side of the Resurrection. Entropy is at work and we have to deal with it.

Entropy is also at work in your Garden of Happiness. If you plant the seeds, water them, then go away for a while, you will come back, not to a garden of delight, but to a garden grown over with weeds that are choking out the things you planted. Jesus told a parable to his disciples about plants and weeds. He says that a sower went out to sow seeds one day and some seeds "fell among thorns, which grew up and choked the plants."[2] When he explained the parable, he told the disciples, "The one who received the seed that fell among the thorns is the man who hears the word, but the worries of his life and the deceitfulness of wealth choke it, making it unfruitful."[3]

Weeds sneak into a garden, grow up around the plants, steal the nutrients meant for the plants, and choke them to death. Some weeds are obviously bad - "the worries of life," Jesus calls them. Some do not

---

[2] Matthew 13.7

[3] Matthew 13.22

appear bad at all, and in fact look pretty and are appealing. Wealth, for example, sounds like a pretty and appealing thing, but the weed Jesus refers to isn't wealth itself, it is "the deceitfulness of wealth" - the *idea* that wealth is going to answer all my problems and bring me true happiness. So there are "bad" weeds and "good" weeds - weeds that are obviously nasty and need to be rooted out, and weeds that are deceptively attractive and still need to be rooted out.

An entire book could be written about the "bad" weeds that grow up in our gardens. Saint Paul gives a list that will keep you busy for a while. In Galatians he lists the "acts of sinful nature": "sexual immorality, impurity and debauchery; idolatry and witchcraft; hatred, discord, jealousy, fits of rage, selfish ambition, dissensions, factions and envy; drunkenness, orgies, and the like."[4] About half this list is firmly frowned upon by Christians, and about half this list is more subtle. While good Christian folk obviously take a stand against things like idolatry and sexual immorality, those same folk are blind to the weeds of jealousy and selfish ambition, but they are all weeds that will keep good fruit from growing in our gardens.

For the rest of this chapter I am going to draw your attention to only two "bad" weeds that are particularly threatening to your garden.

---

[4] Galatians 3.19

The Weed of No Pain

I have a confession to make. I hate pain. I especially hate pain caused by dentists. When I was a little boy (back before the days of malpractice lawsuits) I went to a dentist who drank too much. He pulled the wrong tooth and it hurt. He gave me laughing gas to which I had a negative reaction. It left me extremely nauseated for days. Years later, as an adult, I discovered that I was allergic to nitrous oxide: I visited a dentist, was given the gas, and ended up in a fetal position with really bad hallucinations! Consequently, I have avoided dentists like the plague. Until recently, that is, when I found a good dentist who did good work and didn't give me the funny stuff; but get this: I had five, F-I-V-E root canals in one day just to catch up with years of avoiding the dentist.

> *Nobody in their right mind likes pain. But it is a reality and we have to learn to deal with it.*

Nobody in their right mind likes pain. Everyone wants to avoid it. However, pain is a reality and a necessary part of life. The old sports adage is true, "No Pain, No Gain."

One of the weeds that threatens the Garden of Happiness is the notion that we should never have to suffer pain in life. We want our fortunes, we want happiness, we want a good life, but if it means having to suffer to get it, we just give up and walk away.

Psalm 126 is a song of praise and thanksgiving about the Children of Israel returning from captivity. The first verses sing out,

> When the Lord brought back the captives to Zion,
> we were like men who dreamed.
> Our mouths were filled with laughter,
> our tongues with songs of joy.
> Then it was said among the nations,
> "The Lord has done great things for them,"
> The Lord has done great things for us,
> and we are filled with joy.

God is in the work of restoration, and it is his pleasure to bless his children, but the last verses of the psalm ring out the reality:

> Those who sow in tears
> will reap with songs of joy.
> He who goes out weeping,
> carrying seed to sow,
> will return with songs of joy,
> carrying sheaves with him.

Sometimes planting a garden is hard work and involves tears. My grandfather was an old North Texas farmer who spent his life getting up at four in the morning to milk the cows before heading off to his factory job. I can't remember a time when he didn't have cows to milk and horses to care for. I can't remember a time when he didn't have a big garden and hay to bale and potatoes to dig. He used to pay me a nickel a bale for hauling hay, and I hated that job. It would be a hundred degrees and muggy, and we would be throwing bales up onto the trailer as it drove through the field, and with every toss upward there would be hay falling back down on our sweat-drenched bodies. With aching muscles and itching skin we looked forward to a good shower more than to the five-cents-a-bale waiting for us at the end of the day. However, my experience of pain was nothing compared to his own, and others of his generation who spent their days in the hay fields or cotton fields doing the hard work necessary for a little gain. No Pain, No Gain.

The Psalmist knew the truth: "Those who sow in tears will reap with songs of joy." In ancient Israel, when times were tough, there might be just enough grain to either sow, or bake into bread, but not enough for both. So a scarce amount would be set aside for food, and with aching bellies the people would go out and sow grain that could instead fill their hungering stomachs. They sowed in tears. But when harvest came, and there was a bumper crop, the tears turned to

62

laughter. These godly folk would go out to their fields "weeping, carrying seed to sow," but a few months later would return from those same fields "with songs of joy, carrying sheaves" with them.

James, the brother of Jesus, tells us to "consider it pure joy...whenever you face trials of many kinds."[5] This goes against the grain of our comfort and seems unnatural, but it is in those difficult times that we learn to trust in God and he forms us into the men and women he has called us to be. James tells us we should look at adverse situations with a sense of joy "because you know that the testing of your faith develops perseverance. Perseverance must finish its work so that you may be mature and complete, *not lacking anything.*"[6] To reach the place of "not lacking anything" we must live through the times of trials and testing, and the only way to successfully make it through those times is to face them with a resolute and determined joy - knowing that God is going to bring out of our pain a harvest of happiness and goodness.

Don't ever think that raising a crop is easy. If you want happiness in life, you have to work for it. Pluck up the weed of "no pain" before it even gets roots set, because it will choke out your whole garden.

---

[5] James 1.2

[6] James 1.3,4

The Weed of Victim Mentality

Joe Walsh, from *The Eagles*, is one of the great rock guitarists of our time. He has lived a life of debauchery and has found himself at the end of his rope after a long bout with drug and alcohol addiction. When he finally kicked that demon off his shoulders he wrote a beautiful song called *One Day At A Time* in which he recounts how God and friends saw him through to freedom. However, Joe didn't take the victim mentality of blaming his ills on others. Part of the Twelve Step program he went through includes accepting responsibility for the bad choices made. Back in the 90's The Eagles had a hit song, *Get Over It*. It served as something of an anthem against the victim mentality that has become so pervasive in our society.

> The victim mentality asserts that my life is a mess and somebody else should fix it.

I turn on the tube, what do I see?
A whole lotta people crying "Don't blame me."
They point their crooked little fingers at everybody
    else,
Spend all their time feeling sorry for themselves.

Victim of this, victim of that,
Your momma's too thin, and your daddy's too fat.

You say you haven't been the same
Since you had your little crash
But you might feel better
If they gave you some cash...

Get over it!
Get over it!
All this whining and crying and pitching a fit -
Get over it!
Get over it![7]

The victim mentality asserts that my life is a mess
and it's all someone else's fault. I shouldn't have to do
anything to fix my life, others owe it to me to fix my life
for me. I have been cheated or hurt or abused or
wounded, and so others should take care of me and
provide me with all I need to be happy in this life.

The victim mentality is the opposite of the
"bootstrap" mentality that says, "I'm down and out,
stuck at the bottom, but I've got to grab hold of my own
bootstraps and pull myself up." I have never known
anyone with the victim mentality who ever moved
forward in life and experienced true happiness. I have

---

[7] *Get Over It*, lyrics by Don Henley and Glenn Frey, from *The Eagles*
album *Hell Freezes Over*, 1994

known *many* with the bootstrap mentality who started at the bottom, took responsibility for their own problems, did the hard work of recovery, and came out on top.

Part of that bootstrap mentality does indeed include connecting with others who will support you and encourage you and help you, but if you go through life thinking others *owe* you happiness, you will never achieve true happiness. St. Paul was a bootstrap kind of guy. He could have grumbled and complained about all the bad things that happened to him. After he became a believer, he was rejected by his peers (some think even by his own wife), he was persecuted, he was stoned nearly to death, he was chased all across the world - one time a group of zealous Judaizers even pledged to not eat until they had killed him (I wonder if they kept their pledge!). But when Paul was writing to the struggling church in the Greek town of Thessalonica, he told them they too had to become bootstrap Christians: "Make it your ambition to lead a quiet life, to *mind your own business* and to *work with your hands*, just as we told you, so that your daily life may win the respect of outsiders and so that you will *not be dependent on anybody*."[8]

Another of the churches that Paul ministered to was in Ephesus, and apparently they had some converted thieves in the congregation. His admonition to them was, "He who has been stealing must steal no longer,

---

[8] 1 Thessalonians 4.11f

but must work, doing something useful with his own hands, that he may have something to share with those in need."[9]

A person with the victim mentality will always expect others to take care of him. Instead, Paul says, we ought to take care of our own problems and in fact work ourselves into a situation where we can be a blessing to others. As a pastor I have counseled many people with the victim mentality. One of the surest ways to get free from it is to get our eyes off ourselves and onto the needs of others. A person with a victim mentality is so locked into his own problems (and so dependent on others to take care of him) that he can never contribute anything to the greater cause. Here is my challenge to you. If you find this particular weed growing in your Garden of Happiness, root it out by industriousness and a commitment to help others in their need.

A victim looks at the world and says, "I can't be happy because of what has happened to me. I can't be successful unless others make me successful. My joy, my happiness, my blessings, are out of my hands and under the control of others." A victim says, "I am controlled by my past." A *victor*, on the other hand, says, "I am controlled by my future. I can make something of my life no matter what hand has been dealt to me."

---

[9] Ephesians 4.28

Saint Paul was a victor, not a victim. He wrote, "Not that I have already obtained all this, or have already been made perfect, but I press on to take hold of that for which Christ Jesus took hold of me. Brothers, I do not consider myself yet to have taken hold of it. But one thing I do: *Forgetting what is behind* and *straining toward what is ahead*, I press on toward the goal to win the prize for which God has called me heavenward in Christ Jesus."[10]

> Saint Paul was a victor, not a victim. A victim looks to the past, a victor looks to the future.

A victim looks at the past and says, "I can't be happy unless others make me happy." A victor looks to the future and says, "I can be happy because God enables me to rise above external things. It is God's design for me to walk in joy and fulfillment." Again, that victor Paul wrote, "I know what it is to be in need, and I know what it is to have plenty. I have learned the secret of being content in any situation, whether well fed or hungry, whether living in plenty or in want. *I can do everything through him who gives me strength*."[11] Indeed,

---

[10] Philippians 3.12ff

[11] Philippians 4.12f

Paul writes, "In all things we are *more than conquerors* through him who loved us."[12]

In this chapter we have looked at two "ugly" weeds that will choke out the happy plants of our garden: the idea of "no pain" and the victim mentality. In the next chapter we will give our attention to some even more lethal weeds, weeds that *appear* to be beautiful and good but will actually destroy the good things God has in store for us.

---

[12] Romans 8.37

Chapter Four

"Pretty" Weeds

Roses are red,
Violets are blue;
But they don't get around
Like the dandelions do.
-Slim Acres

When my children were younger I had a vegetable garden in the yard, and they liked to help me work the garden. It was a delightful experience planting crops and seeing the process through the eyes of a child. We would plant the seeds, and mark the rows with the seed packets so they could know what to expect to grow. After only a day or two of waiting they began wondering when the seeds were going to sprout and when the fruit was going to bear. One of the interesting things about gardening with kids was sometimes they didn't want me to pull up a weed because it was "pretty," I knew the weed was destructive to the garden plants, but the kids were just attracted to the bright purple or yellow flower born by the weed.

No matter how pretty a weed is, it sucks away the nutrients and life from the plants in your garden. Pretty weeds are all the more dangerous, because in the Garden of Happiness these weeds become substitutes for the true plants and eventually bring about ruin. There are three pretty weeds that are of particular danger to our gardens.

The Weed of Success

Some people think happiness cannot be achieved until they attain "success." Of course, success is measured differently by different folk. "I will be happy if I can just make $50,000 a year." But when that goal is reached it isn't enough so the mantra becomes, "I will be happy if I can make $100,000 a year." But that doesn't bring happiness either. "OK, $125,000 a year and then I will be happy." For other people, the measure of success is not money, but fame, or accomplishment. In any case, this kind of success becomes the proverbial carrot in front of the horse. The horse is driven forward, but he never reaches true happiness because the carrot is always fleeting and fleeing.

Dennis Prager is a practicing Jew and a talk show host who devotes every Friday's show to the subject of happiness. He has written what I consider to be the best book on the subject.[1] Dennis points out that the problem with this mindset is three missing letters: I-E-R. It is wrong to say, "I will be happy if I can just...." It is right to say, "I will be happier if I can just..." If you can't achieve happiness *before* reaching some goal, you won't achieve happiness *after* reaching that goal. Success, however it is measured, cannot be the foundation of happiness. It must be the result of happiness (and hard work). There's nothing wrong with saying, "I will be happier when I get a new job," but there is everything wrong with saying, "I will be happy when I get a new job."

> *Dennis Prager points out that it is wrong to say something will make you happy, but it is right to say something will make you happier.*

We all know people who "have it all" and are not happy. An icon of this mindset is Hollywood. Those people are *messed up*! So many of the Hollywood set are successful by the world's standard - they have money, fame, the jet-set life, yet they are killing themselves,

---

[1] *Happiness is a Serious Problem* by Dennis Prager, New York, Harper/Collins, 1998

drugging themselves and acting out their pain with all kinds of bizarre behavior.

The Psalmist warns us, "Though your riches increase, do not set your hearts on them."[2] When success becomes a *substitute* for happiness, people will be neither happy, nor in the long run successful. It is God's desire for his people to walk in bounty and favor, but the minute we set our hearts on riches and success they become idols in our lives, and the good things that God gives us end up becoming destructive. One of the saddest stories in the Bible is about a bronze serpent which God commanded Moses to make. The people had been bitten by poisonous snakes, and they had only to look upon the serpent on the pole and they were healed! [3] This prefigured the very image of Christ lifted up on the cross bringing healing to all, but just a few generations later God judged the people of Israel for having turned the bronze serpent into an idol.[4] They were worshiping a good thing that God had given them, and it brought them destruction! The book of Proverbs tells us, "Whoever trusts in his riches will fall, but the righteous will thrive like a green leaf."[5]

---

[2] Psalm 62.10

[3] Numbers 21.4-8

[4] 2 Kings 18.1-5

[5] Proverbs 11.28

Remember the parable of the Sower and the Seeds? Jesus said that the word was planted in the hearts of some, but it wasn't just the "worries of this life" that choked out the Word of God, it was also the "deceitfulness of wealth and the *desire for other things*."[6]

My father is a missionary in Mexico, and is always amazed at how people who have next to nothing can possess true, deep seated happiness, and yet others back home who "have it all" are miserable.

Have you heard the story about the Mexican fisherman?

A yatch docked in a tiny Mexican village and an American tourist stepped off the luxury craft. He complimented a Mexican fisherman on the quality of his fish and asked how long it took him to catch them.

"Not very long," answered the Mexican.

"But then, why didn't you stay out longer and catch more?" asked the American.

The Mexican explained that his small catch was sufficient to meet his needs and those of his family.

---

[6] Mark 4.18

The American asked, "But what do you do with the rest of your time?"

"I sleep late, fish a little, play with my children, and take a siesta with my wife. In the evenings, I go into the village to see my friends, have a few drinks, play the guitar, and sing a few songs. I have a full life."

The American interrupted, "I have an MBA from Harvard and I can help you! You should start by fishing longer every day. You can then sell the extra fish you catch. With the extra revenue, you can buy a bigger boat."

"And after that?" asked the Mexican.

"With the extra money the larger boat will bring, you can buy a second one and a third one and so on until you have an entire fleet of trawlers. Instead of selling your fish to a middle man, you can then negotiate directly with the processing plants and maybe even open your own plant. You can then leave this little village and move to Mexico City, Los Angeles, or even New York City! From there you can direct your huge new enterprise."

"How long would that take?" asked the Mexican.

"Twenty, perhaps twenty-five years," replied the American.

"And after that?"

"Afterwards? Well my friend, that's when it gets really interesting," answered the American, laughing. "When your business gets really big, you can start buying and selling stocks and make millions!"

"Millions? Really? And after that?" asked the Mexican.

"After that you'll be able to retire, live in a tiny village near the coast, sleep late, play with your children, catch a few fish, take a siesta with your wife and spend your evenings drinking and enjoying your friends."

The truth is, success, measured by worldly standards, can actually frustrate true happiness. Please understand that I am not advocating that Christians should be poor and downtrodden. The plan of God is for his people to be lenders, not borrowers, to be the head and not the tail,[7] but even success as a gift from God can become a snare that leads to our downfall.

---

[7] Deuteronomy 28.12-14

The Weed of Fun

Happiness and fun are not the same thing. Some people spend their lives in pursuit of fun thinking it will bring them happiness. There are two kinds of fun. The first, honestly, is the kind of fun you ought not have: sinful fun. Don't ever let people tell you that sin is not fun. It is. That's why so many people sin! But sinful fun only leads to death.

Saint Peter wrote, "For you have spent enough time in the past doing what pagans choose to do - living in debauchery, lust, drunkenness, orgies, carousing and detestable idolatry. They think it strange that you do not plunge with them into the same flood of dissipation, and they heap abuse on you. But they will have to give account to him who is ready to judge the living and the dead."[8] Eugene Peterson paraphrased the text like this: "You've already put in your time in that God-ignorant way of life, partying night after night, a drunken and profligate life. Now it's time to be done with it for good. Of course, your old friends don't understand why you don't join in with the old gang anymore. But you don't have to give an account to them. They're the ones who will be called on the carpet - and before God himself."[9]

---

[8] 1 Peter 4.3-5

[9] 1 Peter 4.3-5, *The Message: The Bible in Contemporary Language* by Eugene Peterson, Colorado Springs, NavPress, 2004

People pursue these things, which Paul calls "deeds of the flesh"[10], searching for happiness, but not finding it because these things are temporary and happiness is rooted in things eternal. Shakespeare defined lust as "past reason wanted, no sooner had, past reason hated." Have you known people who pursued the deeds of the flesh looking for happiness, and having no sooner embraced these deeds of darkness found themselves hating them? How many people have pursued sexual affairs only to find that their dream of a romantic whirl turned out to be a nightmare from hell? How many people have pursued alcohol as a means to fun, only to find themselves hating what they'd done the next morning? How many people have played with drugs as an avenue to fun, only to find their lives ruined by an addictive monster?

When people pursue "the deeds of the flesh", what they really yearn for is true happiness in God.

Paul tells us that those who practice (keep on doing) these kinds of things "will not inherit the kingdom of

---

[10] Galatians 5.19

God."[11] This is not an angry prophet threatening hell to bad boys and girls, this is a spiritual father telling his Christian children that the things they are doing will not bring about what they are looking for. When Christians pursue these deeds of the flesh, what are they really looking for? What is it that will truly fill the hole in their hearts? Three things: to be accepted by God, to have peace in their souls, and to have joy (or happiness). Why, this is the very definition of the kingdom of God! Paul tells us that the kingdom of God, is "righteousness, peace and joy in the Holy Spirit."[12] Keep doing these fleshly things, he says, and you won't inherit the kingdom of God. Keep doing these destructive things, and you'll never find what you're really looking for. People who keep doing these things will never find true happiness, because they are allowing the weed of fun to crowd out the true plants of joy.

"But I don't do *those* things," you might reply, "girls just wanna have fun." You need to know that there are all kinds of fun that are not evil, but are still substitutes for happiness. Good Christian folk who would *never* embrace these "deeds of the flesh" can still find happiness choked out of their lives by the substitution of good and fun things. Good is often the enemy of best. There are things God has planned for your life that you may never achieve because you settle for good instead of

---

[11] Galatians 5.21

[12] Romans 14.17

best. Happiness is best. Fun is good. Some people will never reach happiness because they have settled for fun - not bad fun - not drunkenness and carousing and such, but temporary enjoyments that distract from deep happiness.

Do you know people who are the life of the party, always on the go, always looking for the next fun thing, but when you stand back and look at their lives you see this huge hole of emptiness in their soul? Fun is not a means to happiness. It can be a poor substitute for happiness that prevents us from ever achieving the real deal. Christians *ought* to have fun, but not at the expense of happiness. When fun gets in the way of happiness, it becomes a weed in the garden.

The Weed of More

The final pretty weed we will look at is the weed of More. It is a relative of the weeds of Success and Fun. "If I could just have more money or food or drink or sex or drugs or study or prayer or church or friends or..." "If I could just have more, I would be happy." Again, we must learn the lesson from Dennis Prager: it is alright to say, "If I could have more I would be happ*ier*." but it is wrong to say, "If I could have more I could be happy."

The antidote to the weed of more is to develop the quality of contentment. Contentment is not a laisse-faire attitude toward life. Contentment is not a happy-go-lucky, que sera sera outlook. Contentment is not simply being *satisfied* with whatever hand life has dealt you. Contentment is understanding that no matter what you face, you can be at peace and have happiness.

Saint Paul tells us that "godliness with contentment is great gain."[13] Paul knew what it was like to be wealthy and what it was like to be poor. He knew what it meant to be full and what it meant to be hungry. Now obviously, he would rather be full than hungry, and he would rather abound than be abased. But no matter where he found himself in life, he wrote, "I have learned the secret of being content in any and every situation."[14]

Christians ought to strive for excellence. There's nothing wrong with wanting more. It is a God-given quality in the soul of humans that drives them to productivity and improvement for themselves and for others. When I was a child my favorite church song was also a horribly erroneous one:

> I'm satisfied with, just a cottage below,
> A little silver, and a little gold.
> But in that city, where the ransomed will shine,
> I want a mansion, that's silver-lined.[15]

---

[13] 1 Timothy 6.6

[14] Philippians 4.12

[15] *Mansion Over the Hilltop* by Ira F. Stanphill, 1949

All our hopes were on the hereafter. We were looking for deliverance from this world and the fulfillment of our wildest dreams in the next. This is not at all what the Bible teaches. This is actually the result of the slave mentality of the nineteenth century where poor black slaves had little or no hope in this life and looked instead to the life to come. "Swing low, sweet chariot, coming for to carry me home" (also, by the way, a coded reference to the Underground Railroad). It trickled down from that era to the next few generations of Evangelical and Pentecostal Christians who found themselves on "the wrong side of the tracks" and were considered "outcasts." The message became, "Don't expect much of anything good in this life, just keep thinking about heaven." Slavery was evil then and it is evil now, but a slave mentality is not the mind that God gives to his children. Are there times when things are so bad that people need deliverance? Certainly! However, even in the worst of situations, the mind of the believer ought to be set on victory and conquest, not only in the next life, but in this one too!

For some Christians, all their hopes are on the hereafter. This is not what the Bible teaches.

So contentment is not the same as satisfaction. I can be content in bad situations, but not satisfied. I can accept the situation and have true happiness in the midst of difficulties, all the while working for the betterment of that situation. The problem with many modern Christians, however, is that they have neither satisfaction *nor* contentment. The writer of Hebrews admonishes us, "Keep your lives free from the love of money and be content with what you have, because God has said, 'Never will I leave you; never will I forsake you.'"[16] Isn't it amazing that so many Christians know and can quote the last half of that sentence, "I will never leave you nor forsake you," and yet are oblivious to the first half, "be content with what you have"?

God's desire is to bless his people. Job tells us, "If they obey and serve God, they will spend the rest of their days in prosperity and their years in contentment."[17]

There are lots of things I want. I want an unabridged set of the Oxford English Dictionary. I want to teach the Bible in Mexico. I want to write more books that will make a difference in people's lives. I want the church I serve to thrive like never before. I want a boat. As long as I'm dreaming, I want a little

---

[16] Hebrews 13.5

[17] Job 36.10

cottage - doesn't have to be a mansion - just a tiny cottage...on the Caribbean! But I don't need these things to attain happiness. I'm not saying you shouldn't want more. I'm saying you shouldn't want more in order to be happy. If that's the case, More is just a weed.

Chapter Five

Cultivating: The Work That Needs To Be Done

Our England is a garden,
and such gardens are not made
By singing: "Oh, how beautiful!"
and sitting in the shade,
While better men than we go out
and start their working lives
At grubbing weeds from gravel-paths
with broken dinner-knives.
-Rudyard Kipling

Gardens don't just happen. We have already discovered that gardens are not natural, they are works of art. Leave nature to itself and it is beautiful from a distance but can be deadly up close. There are snakes that will poison you and avalanches that will crush you and heat waves that will dehydrate you and blizzards that will freeze you and lightning that will fry you and bears and bugs and fish that will eat you! If you find yourself in the middle of nature somewhere, hungry and thirsty and lost, and you come upon a little cottage with a pretty garden, your first response will be, "Thank God! Someone is here!" Cottages and gardens don't just spring up unattended. Such things take work.

After God had done the initial work of planting the Garden of Eden we read, "There was no man to work the ground," so "the Lord God took the man and put him in the Garden of Eden to work it and take care of it."[1] Did you notice the dirty four-letter word? *W-O-R-K*. Work is not a curse. The curse placed on Adam was that his work would be difficult, "through painful toil...by the sweat of your brow."[2]

Other translations say to *cultivate* the garden, and cultivate is an interesting English word (with a Latin root). It means to *care* for the garden, but we also get the word *cult* from it. Anymore when we hear the word cult we think of religious crazies saying weird things and acting bizarre, but any good dictionary will tell you that cult simply means the particular religious worship of a given people. It has to do with the *work* people do in worship. One enduring connection to the word is that most Christian churches still call what they do on Sunday morning their "worship *service*."

---

[1] Genesis 2.5, 15

[2] Genesis 3.17ff

The Ground Must Be Worked

Some Christians have the silly notion that just because they believe in Christ, everything should come to them on a silver platter. "I'll just follow God and *he* will take care of everything for me!"

I have known people (I could tell you their names, but I won't), who believed they were called to great things in the ministry. They believed that God was raising them up to be pastors of great churches, or evangelists with worldwide ministries. But they never did anything about it, and they never accomplished their dreams. I don't doubt that God could have called them to great things indeed, but one of the very reasons God created man in the first place was to *work*! Happiness doesn't just happen. If you want happiness in your life you will have to work for it. Gardens don't just spring up on their own. The ground has to be tilled. The weeds (remember them?) have to be weeded. The plants have to be planted. And trained. And watered. And fertilized. And harvested.

The Bible is often much more practical and "this-worldly" than we would like it to be. The old heresy of Gnosticism taught the only thing that really matters is the spiritual. The Gnostics taught that true salvation is achieved by getting free from the physical. Sadly, Gnosticism is still hanging around in much of what passes for Christian thinking. For example, too many

Christians believe Christ came to take us to heaven, and too much evangelism asks, "If you were to die tonight do you know where you would spend eternity?" Christ didn't come to take us to heaven. He came to bring us into the New Creation - a rebirthed "heavens and earth."[3] In fact, the new creation has already begun in the resurrection of Christ and the new birth of Christians[4] (but that is for another book). Gnostics taught that God wanted to free us from the physical so we could have a purely spiritual life. True Christianity teaches us that God is redeeming the physical, and that even in the end, our physical bodies shall be raised incorruptible and be clothed with immortality. [5]

> *Too many Christians believe that Christ came to take us to heaven. He didn't. He came to bring the New Creation.*

God cares about "stuff." He cares about the world. He cares about the physical. In the incarnation, he joined himself *to* the physical forever. All that to say that

---

[3] Isaiah 65.17

[4] 2 Corinthians 5.17

[5] 1 Corinthians 15.20ff, but read the entire chapter.

part of working out our own salvation, our own wholeness and healing and happiness, involves, well, just that: *working*! God made us creatures of spirit and body and our godly work is both spiritual and physical. Some Christians seem to think that God will just do everything for them and they won't have to lift a finger to accomplish his will and purpose. They think their Garden of Happiness should just bloom and blossom all on its own, but that is not the way gardens grow. In that most practical (and physical) of books, Proverbs tells us, "He who *works* his land will have abundant food, but he who chases fantasies lacks judgment."[6]

The Work Never Ends

Let me tell you what I think would be the perfect system of gardening. I would get up one cool spring morning, go out to the freshly tilled soil, plant the seeds, and sit back in my porch chair with a nice iced tea and watch them grow. That's all. Nothing else. In no time at all I would have a cornucopia of delightful vegetables for my own table, and the tables of my friends. Little blue birds would circle about my head and start singing while the forest animals came and danced around me. Because *that*, my friend, is a fairy tale!

---

[6] Proverbs 12.11

The reality is that gardening is work from beginning to end. The work doesn't end when the crop is planted. In fact, it has only just begun, so farming requires diligence and patience and setting in for the long haul.

> You can't just plant a seed and expect everything to come up roses. The work never ends.

Saint James was the Bishop of Jerusalem and the brother of Jesus. He oversaw the church during a time of great persecution and scattering. When he wrote his epistle he was writing to the pastors of his scattered congregation who found themselves having to start all over outside of Jerusalem. It would have been an easy time to give up, to quit the ministry and go back to working at the butcher shop. James knew that deliverance was around the corner (Jerusalem was about to be destroyed by "the Lord's coming" and the persecutors of the Christians were about to be out of the picture), but he also knew these folk needed to hang in there. So he wrote, "Be patient, then, brothers, until the Lord's coming. See how the farmer waits for the land to yield its valuable crop and how patient he is for the autumn and spring rains."[7]

---

[7] James 5.7

One of the characteristics of godliness applauded throughout the Scriptures by everyone from Moses to Peter is *endurance*. God wants you to be happy. He also wants to prosper you. However, things take time and he calls us to endure until we achieve our goal.

The San Antonio Spurs is the best basketball team in the history of the sport (no, I'm not prejudiced, they're just really good and happen to be my favorite team)). In the locker room of the Spurs there are plaques with a quote from Jacob Riis, translated into every language represented on the team, including English, Spanish, French and German: "When nothing seems to help, I go look at a stonecutter hammering away at his rock perhaps a hundred times without as much as a crack showing in it. Yet at the hundred and first blow it will split in two, and I know it was not that blow that did it, but all that had gone before."

If you are going to be successful in your Garden of Happiness, you can't just do the work of planting and then wait for everything to come up roses. You must dig in. For the long haul. You must endure and be faithful. You must not be easily set back by unexpected difficulties. If inclement weather sets in (adverse situations you face in daily life) you must deal with it, but don't give up, and you will harvest the fruit of happiness.

The Good Way To Want More

In the last chapter we saw that one of the pretty weeds that often infiltrates our Gardens of Happiness is the weed of more. More becomes a weed that chokes out true happiness when we think we would finally be happy if only we had more of this thing or the other. We saw that there is a blessedness in being content while striving for greater accomplishments.

> God created humans with an insatiable nature, a blessing of dissatisfaction.

However, God also created humans with an insatiable nature, a *blessing of dissatisfaction*.[8] The difference between the weed of wanting more and the blessing of dissatisfaction is whether we think more will make us happy, or make us happier. God placed in our very nature a desire to achieve. Our heroes are those who have achieved in spite of

---

[8] Cf. Prager, p. 19

staggering odds against them.[9] Betterment is part of our nature; to have more, to give more, to serve more. Human dissatisfaction has led to the cure of diseases, the liberating of slaves, the creation of better societies, beautiful art, the invention of new technologies in science and medicine, in short, the *improvement* of life. Hebrews 11 is called "The Hebrews Hall of Faith" and it lists the stories of men and women of God who, through faith, "conquered kingdoms, administered justice...shut the mouths of lions, quenched the fury of the flames, escaped the edge of the sword; whose weakness was turned into strength; and who became powerful in battle and routed foreign armies."[10] Not the kind of things you would expect from complacent people with no vision for betterment. The Christian faith has become fertile ground for invention and exploration and civilization and productivity. Men and women of God have throughout history, in hope of *more* and *betterment*, done the hard *work* necessary to achieve greatness.

---

[9] I recommend to you the inspiring story of Sir Ernest Shackleton, who survived a disastrous expedition to Antarctica aboard his ship named, appropriately enough, *The Endurance*. Several books tell the story, but one of the best is *The Endurance: Shackleton's Legendary Anarctic Expedition*, by Caroline Alexander, New York, Knopf, 1988. This edition of Shackleton's story includes stunning black and white photography by the expedition photographer, Frank Hurley.

[10] Hebrews 11.33ff, but consider the entire chapter.

The word *better* is used 129 times in the Bible. Better is a qualitative word, and Scripture is full of telling us that one thing is better than another thing. God wants things to be better, and so should we! However, achieving betterment takes work. It takes cultivation. It takes ongoing tinkering and experimenting. It takes endurance. Although we ought to be happy and content, we are still called by God to make things better; it's how he designed us.

The writer of Ecclesiastes tells us, "I know that there is nothing better for men than to be happy and to do good while they live."[11] This is foundational thinking. This is the key to the Garden of Happiness - to be happy and do good. However, the writer continues, "That everyone may eat and drink, and find satisfaction in all his toil - this is the gift of God." God desires for you to be happy, and happier. He desires for you to be blessed, and to be more blessed, but it doesn't come automatically. It comes to those who commit their ways to the Lord, roll up their sleeves, and determine to do the work of cultivating in the Garden of Happiness. Hi ho, hi ho, it's off to work we go.

---

[11] Ecclesiastes 3.12

Chapter Six

Some Plants in the Garden

What oxygen is to the lungs,
such is hope to the meaning of life.
-Emil Brunner

There are all kinds of different gardens. There are flower gardens and herb gardens and vegetable gardens. There are formal gardens and informal gardens. Once, during a busy time in my life when I couldn't have a full garden, I planted a pico de gallo garden: jalapeños, tomatoes, onions and cilantro - ready made fresh hot sauce. Some people have expansive back yards with gardens big enough to feed an army. Some people living in big-city high-rises have gardens in boxes growing on their balconies. But one thing all gardens have in common is plants.

There are many different plants to be planted in the Garden of Happiness - for a complete list just study the characteristics of godly men and women throughout the Bible - but in the next two chapters we will give our attention to a few essential plants that every Garden of Happiness needs. This chapter will focus on two *attitudes*, and the next chapter will focus on three *actions*.

Meaning and Purpose

Large corporations spend tens of thousands of dollars developing vision statements. The final statement may be only a sentence or two, but an enormous amount of money, man-hours, thought, discussion and energy goes into producing it. A vision statement is important to a company because it gives definition to the company's purpose, and a company without a purpose will not long remain a company. Churches are the same way. Their vision statement may be well crafted and in print, or it may be related word of mouth among the members of the congregation, but a church that doesn't know why it is there will not have a successful ministry. The same is true of people. People who know their purpose can spend their lives striving to accomplish particular and unique goals that are in keeping with their life-purpose. People who don't know their purpose get up in the morning, go to work, come home in the evening, plop down in front of the TV or internet, go to bed, and get up the next morning and do the same thing. In short order they find their lives boring, without direction and going nowhere. People without purpose end up in a state of either resignation or despair.

Proverbs tells us, "Where there is no vision, the people perish."[12] The word *perish* means to cast off restraint, or to run around in circles. Have you ever been lost in the woods or on the road? Have you ever walked or driven for a good long while only to end up where you started? That can be a very frustrating experience, and if you're in the wilderness it can be a very dangerous experience too! This sort of "lostness" also happens in people's lives. Sometimes people will wander through life without a sense of direction or purpose, and five years down the road find themselves right back where they started. They will get out of a bad marriage only to find themselves in another bad marriage. They will be put all their energy into a friendship, find themselves betrayed by that friend, but then experience the same kind of thing the next go around.

If you don't have a vision in life you will just run around in circles.

This is exactly what happened with the people of Israel after they had been led out of Egypt by Moses. Exodus tells the story of the people losing vision: it happened when Moses sent spies ahead of the people

---

[12] Proverbs 29.18, KJV

into the land God had promised to give them, to discover the lay of the land and find out what kind of inhabitants were there. The spies came back saying, "No way, Moses! We can't take the land! Those guys living there now are *big*! Why, we look like grasshoppers compared to them!" It is noteworthy that they didn't look like grasshoppers in the eyes of their enemies, but "we seemed like grasshoppers in our own eyes."[13] The book of Numbers records that these spies sent the bad report among all the people, discouraging them and causing them to lose faith. The people lost their vision. They lost their sense of purpose. The end result was that none of them (save two - Joshua and Caleb) entered into the land that God had promised to them. They had to wander in the wilderness until that generation died off so the next generation could lay hold of the vision and cross over in conquest.

Perhaps the first and most important plant in a Garden of Happiness is the plant of purpose; without it the garden just goes to pot, disarray sets in, and not only does true happiness never get cultivated, but life becomes meaningless and void. This plant of purpose come in two varieties. The first is general, and it applies to everyone, the second is specific, and it applies particularly to you.

---

[13] Numbers 13.33

Over the years as a pastor I can't tell you how many times people have talked to me about trying to find their purpose in life. Usually what this means is they want a specific and clear blueprint from God that details every step of their lives from the present moment until their last day. These folk haven't yet learned the principle of working from the general to the specific. It isn't a deep principle, and you would think that people would "get it" right off the bat, but many don't. If you want to learn to play the guitar, you don't begin with the intricacies of Clapton licks or Segovia runs. First you learn chords. Basic chords. G, C and D. Simple stuff. Foundational. General. If you want to learn to cook you don't begin with a complicated French souffle. You start with frying eggs. People tend to understand this when it comes to guitars and cooking, but when it comes to the purpose of life they want God to line it all out for them ahead of time and show them the end from the beginning. That isn't the way God works. He works with our life purpose just like he works with us learning to play the guitar and learning to cook. That is, he tells us, "Start with the basics."

Finding your God-given purpose isn't difficult...if you start with the basics.

The basics, when it comes to purpose, are the general things that are *everybody's* purpose. The Westminster Catechism defines the purpose of every human being in these words: "Man's chief end is to glorify God, and to enjoy him forever." Now, that may seem like pretty basic stuff, and it may seem rather simplistic to you, but let me ask you a question: As you sit down to discover your life's purpose, have you *begun* with something this basic? Because before you figure out the specifics of what God is calling you to (oh, say, to marry this particular man or to move to that particular city or to engage in this other particular occupation), you need to plant a few simple general purpose plants in your garden. First, God's purpose for you is to glorify him. Let's begin with that. Are you doing that in your life, *whatever it is* you're doing? Second, are you enjoying God?

The prophet Micah gives us another general, basic vision statement. The King James Version says it best: "He has shown thee, oh man, what is good, and what does the Lord require of thee, but to do justly, and to love mercy, and to walk humbly with thy God."[14]

Before you start figuring out the intricate scales on your spiritual guitar, how about you learn those three basic chords? God's purpose in your life is to do the right thing always. That alone can be a difficult assignment. Then he calls you to be a man or woman of mercy - to *love* mercy. This is even more difficult than

---

[14] Micah 6.8

doing the right thing, because mercy comes into the picture when other people *don't* do the right thing! Finally, you will find your meaning in life as you walk humbly before God. This may be the most difficult of the three, because if you are doing what is right and showing mercy to people who don't do what is right, you might get puffed up and proud and think you are pretty special. So God balances out your purpose by saying the final chord you learn to strum ought to be humility.

These are things all people are called to do. This is purpose in the general sense. This is the place to begin, and I can't stress enough that this *is* the place to begin, so if you haven't begun your Garden of Happiness by planting a row or two of general purpose, go back and do it right away. But this is not the place to end. God has more in store for you than fulfilling the role of a "happy everyman." He has a specific purpose for you as well, but how do you figure out what it is?

First, understand that there are some basic specifics for you, and it doesn't take a rocket scientist to figure them out. If you are married, it is God's purpose in your life for you to be faithful to your spouse. If you are a parent, it is God's purpose in your life for you to love your children and train them up to follow him. If you work at a job, it is God's purpose for you to get along with your boss and give him an honest day's work. It is God's purpose for you to worship him by gathering

103

together with his people. It is God's purpose for you, as much as you are able, to take care of your own needs rather than depending on others. The list goes on forever, and if you would like to find more of these basic specifics for yourself, I suggest just looking at the last half of most of Saint Paul's epistles.[15]

Once you understand some of the basic yet particular purposes that God has called you to, you will also discover that there are some more specific ones. Obviously I can't tell you what they are, because I don't even know who is reading this book, but I can tell you how to find them. I can show you how to find your specific purpose and destiny that God has prepared for you in one easy step. Be faithful in what you already know. Do the little things and the bigger things will come. Do the general things and the specific things will come. Jesus told a parable about a businessman who went on a long journey and entrusted some finances to his servants. He told them to put the money to good use and when he returned he discovered that one servant hadn't obeyed, and two had. To the faithful servants he said, "Well done good and faithful servant! You have been faithful with a few things; I will put you in charge of many things. Come and share your master's

---

[15] Paul had a habit of writing his epistles in two parts. The first half is usually theological, and the second half is usually very practical. There are exceptions to the rule, but this is generally true. For starters, try Ephesians, the last half.

happiness!"[16] How do you share in God's happiness? You work at being faithful in the little things. As you are faithful in the little (and general, and basic) things, God will begin entrusting you with bigger (and more specific) things. You see, God doesn't give us a blueprint. He calls us to take a walk with him. It is one day at a time. He does not show us what is around the corner, he just asks us to be faithful with what we can see now and to trust him in the path. However, he has laid out things in our path ahead of time which are things of purpose[17], and as we are faithful in the now, these future purposes will become more obvious.

Too many people want a specific destiny without honoring the general call already on their lives.

Be careful not to get the cart before the horse. Too many people want a specific sense of destiny with no intention of honoring the general call already upon their lives. Has God called you to be the next Albert Einstein? Fabulous! Start by working on your bachelor's degree in science. Has God called you to be the next Michael W. Smith? Wonderful! Start by taking piano lessons.

---

[16] Matthew 25.21

[17] Ephesians 2.10

Has God called you to be the next Billy Graham? Great! Start by being faithful in church.

Hope

I am convinced that a person cannot be happy without a generally positive outlook on life. How you think ends up being how you act. Proverbs says, "As a man thinketh in his heart, so is he."[18] If, deep in the interior of your heart, you have an ongoing sense of hope - of a positive outlook toward the future - it cannot help but manifest itself through your countenance, your attitude, and your actions.

There are many things in this world that will steal hope. Bad things happen that can send anyone into a tailspin. Tragedies can be devastating and take a long, long time to work through. I'm not being glib and dismissing the pain and devastation of bad things, but too many people automatically enter their future with the anticipation of nothing going right, nothing being good and no sense of hope. I can promise you that those people will *never* be happy.

Have you heard of people talking to their plants? I've never done it, and I think it might be a little (or a lot) silly, but some people insist that talking to plants causes them to thrive. Well, hope is a plant that

---

[18] Proverbs 23.7, KJV

sometimes needs talking to. When the plant of hope is young, it is fragile and any little wind of adversity can harm it. When it is older and stronger it can still be harmed by the storms of life. Sometimes hope needs some words of encouragement. That encouragement might come from a friend of yours, or it might come from yourself. When King David found himself in the mullygrubs he talked to himself, "Why are you downcast, O my soul? Why so disturbed within me? Put your hope in God, for I will yet praise him, my Savior and my God."[19] "But as for me, I will always have hope; I will praise you more and more."[20]

The plant of hope, in order to endure, must have strong roots in a special soil. If hope is planted in another person, it will get hurt. If hope is planted in a political conviction, it will be disappointed. If hope is planted in a church, a pastor, a husband, a wife, a president, a boss, an investment, an economy, a retirement plan or any other temporal thing, it will ultimately fail. The soil which hope must be planted in is the ultimate Ground of Being[21], God himself.

How many times have you been let down by friends? Betrayed by people close to you? Hurt by

---

[19] Psalm 42.5, 11; 43.5

[20] Psalm 71.14

[21] Written with a wink and a nod to Paul Tillich.

spiritual leaders? Abandoned by political parties? If you put your hope in anything from this world it will be fleeting, because the stability of anything from this world is fleeting. If, on the other hand, you put your hope in God, then the storms of life can howl and the winds of adversity can beat against your Garden of Happiness, but you will endure because you are grounded in something eternal.

This is not just spiritual talk that sounds good but has no practical reality. Saint Paul wrote, "We also rejoice in our sufferings, because we know that suffering produces perseverance; perseverance, character; and character, hope. And hope does not disappoint us, because God has poured out his love into our hearts by the Holy Spirit whom he has given us."[22]

> If you have a deep-seated conviction that God is in the mix, you can persevere and come out a champion.

To have happiness, you must have hope, and in order to have enduring hope that survives suffering, it must be rooted in an awareness that God is in the process of working in you no

---

[22] Romans 5.3ff

matter what life hands you. If you have a deep seated conviction that no matter what adversities you face, God is there, in the mix, working in, with, through and for you, with a future goodness that includes this life and the life to come, then you can persevere and come out the other side a champion.

But champions have a view to victory. Jesus told his little ragtag band of twelve followers, "I have told you these things, so that in me you may have peace. In the world you will have trouble. But take heart [KJV: be of good cheer]! I have overcome the world."[23] These twelve went out from Jerusalem into the whole known world (to India, Asia, Spain, Africa, Rome, Greece, Persia and a host of other places), all facing hardships and even martyrdom, yet with happiness and with hope because they knew that the God they served had already won! *Even in defeat, they couldn't be defeated!*

Theologians who use big words tell us that Genesis 3.15 is the *protoevangelion*. Theologians who use little words tell us that Genesis 3.15 is the *first gospel*. It records God's curse upon the serpent (that is, the Devil) in the Garden of Eden, and promises him that a son of Eve will crush his head. We all know that on the cross Jesus crushed the head of the serpent, and in the Resurrection he wrested power from the Devil and took the keys of death and hell. However, the victory of

---

[23] John 16.33

Christ doesn't end with his personal defeat of the enemy. What began in him continues in us. Paul told the Roman Christians, "The God of peace will soon crush Satan under *your* feet."[24]

What could you do if you knew you were invincible? Then do it! God is in the process of crushing Satan under your feet. Even when things go wrong, even when things turn out bad, God is there in the middle of things working them toward goodness for you. He is like a master chess player who sees his opponent's plan about a dozen moves ahead (except with God, he knows the enemy's entire game plan from start to finish). Nothing the opponent does even phases the purposes of God. Saint Paul said it like this: "And we know that *in all things* God works for the good of those who love him, who have been called according to his purpose...If God is for us, who can be against us? He who did not spare his own Son, but gave him up for us all - how will he not also, along with him, graciously give us all things...*In all these things* we are *more than conquerors* through him who loved us."[25]

Church buildings are interesting. The altar area is called the sanctuary (although people tend to call the whole worship space the sanctuary). The area where the congregation worships is called the nave (from the Latin

---

[24] Romans 16.20

[25] Romans 8.28, 31f, 37

110

word meaning boat, because it typically used to look like a boat - and, Noah's Ark is a symbol of the Church), and the outside entrance is called the narthex (which actually means, of all things, the reeds - as in cattails or bulrushes - it represents the world. We leave the world and step into the heavenly realm to worship God, and we go back into the world to love and serve him). At the church I pastor we borrowed an idea from the Russian Orthodox tradition and placed, in the floor of our narthex, a stone etching of a dragon - the devil. He is out there in the world, prowling around looking to do harm. In the old country of Russia the little old grandmothers with muddy boots would walk into the church and step on the head of the serpent as they moved toward worship. In our church, at the end of the service as the congregation departs, the little children often gather and dance upon the head of the dragon, laughing as they stomp. We are raising a generation with hope.

> *In our church the little children gather and dance on the head of the dragon.*

111

Chapter Seven

Some More Plants In the Garden

And remember when you're out there
Tryin' to heal the sick
That you must always
First forgive them.
-Bob Dylan

My grandchildren (Shirley and I have two at the time of this writing, and we hope for many more) have a heritage that I think is very unique. It is not unique to have a grandfather who is a minister; many people can make that claim. Many people can make the claim to have a great-grandfather as a minister too. But Kenny and Elijah lay claim to *all* of their great-grandfathers - all four of them - being ministers of the Gospel. Two of them (my father and my father-in-law) have lived out their lives as missionaries in Mexico, bringing truth and hope to the poorest of the poor and the least of the least. Both of these men are heroes to me. They have lived sacrificial lives, imparted their gifts to others, and have established ministries that will long outlive them and their living memories. They have planted seeds into the fertile soil of the Mexican people that will bear fruit for generations to come. Between the two of them they have established more than 500 churches, several Bible Schools, and a medical clinic that has blossomed into a full-blown hospital.

My father-in-law has left this life and is present with the Lord (he died the same day as Pope John Paul II, and I would love to have seen *that* heavenly meeting!), and my father continues to do the missionary work God has called him to. They are very different men, but other than a passion for missions they share one more thing in common: they are both realists and neither of them gives two hoots for hyper-spiritual people who are always speaking positive confessions and words of blessings while not *doing* anything to make a difference. Nothing drives a missionary crazier than empty super-spiritual talk! I have heard both of them lament the attitudes, words, and non-actions of Christians who visited their harvest fields. My father-in-law used to get peeved about people who told him how much they were going to support missionary work once they had reached a certain

> *Nothing drives a missionary crazier than super-spiritual talk without actions to match.*

financial level in life. He knew (and he was quick to tell them) that if they didn't support missions while they had a modest income, they weren't going to support missions when they struck it rich. My father once had a Charismatic pastor riding with him through a destitute section of a Mexico, extending his hands and speaking blessings of prosperity over the villages. Dad put a stop to it by telling the man that his financial support would be more of a blessing than his empty words. Remember the old adage, "Actions speak louder than words"? It has endured as a saying because it is true.

Good Works

Do you remember when we had a chat about Gnosticism, the early church heresy which taught that God is only interested in the spiritual and not the physical, and that the way to salvation is to *escape* the body? I told you that Gnosticism still has fingers running through much of the Christian world, and this is nowhere more true than in the contemporary inclination to separate spirituality from actions.

Everyone loves the story of God transporting Philip from south of Jerusalem to Azotus after Philip brought the Ethiopian Eunuch to Christ and baptized him.[1] The basic reading is that Philip baptized the Ethiopian, then simply disappeared, and was transported through thin

---

[1] Acts. 8.26-40

air to Azotus where he continued preaching the Gospel. The text says, "When they came up out of the water, the Spirit of the Lord suddenly took Philip away, and the eunuch did not see him again, but went on his way rejoicing." And that may very well have been what happened. I suppose someone could give it a different reading - that Philip said farewell and went on his way and the eunuch never saw him again, but pretty much all Bible commentators, from the early fathers of the Church until now, understand this as something of a miracle.

But have you heard about the time God moved Saint Paul from Asia to Europe? Paul was in Asia Minor (Troas, to be precise) when he had a vision of a man from Macedonia (that would be current day - uh - Macedonia) asking him to come over to Macedonia and bring the Gospel with him.[2] So Paul "got ready at once to leave for Macedonia." Here is how the story goes: "From Troas we put out to sea and sailed straight through to Samothrace, and the next day on to Neapolis. From there we traveled to Philippi, a Roman colony and the leading city of the district of Macedonia." Now, I ask you. Did God move Paul from Troas to Philippi? Of course he did! But it wasn't a poof into the air and a sudden relocation. If indeed God did that with Philip it was the exception and not the rule. God moved Paul by speaking to him by the Spirit and

---

[2] Acts 16. 1-12

from there Paul walking, buying a boat ticket, sailing, and walking some more. Paul sailed and walked a *lot* in his ministry! It didn't seem very spiritual as the blisters wore on his feet, but he was putting his *faith* into *action*; and God was as much in Paul's movement as he was in Philip's movement.

> Saint Paul walked till he had blisters on his feet. He was putting his faith into action!

Don't talk to missionaries about driving through the hovels and speaking words of blessings. They are liable to lose their spiritual cool and smack you a good one! Saint James wrote, "Faith by itself, if it is not accompanied by action, is dead."[3]

If you want true happiness, you're going to have to *do* something to achieve it, and the something that you have to do is *good works*. The Preacher said, "I know that there is nothing better for men than to be happy and *do good* while they live,"[4] and Jesus went so far as to say that we ought to do good even to those who are against us: "But I tell you who hear me: Love your enemies, *do*

---

[3] James 2.17

[4] Ecclesiastes 3.12

117

good to those who hate you."[5] Paul instructed Timothy to "Command them to *do good*, to be *rich in good deeds*, and to be generous and willing to share,"[6] and the writer of Hebrews tells us "do not forget to *do good* and share with others, for with such sacrifices God is pleased."[7]

You may have noticed that all these texts imply that good works are done to others. Some Christians get so focused on their own selves that all they can think about, when it comes to spirituality, is how much they pray, read and study Scripture, fast, and don't sin. But all these things are related to the self. The Bible teaches that just as important (and perhaps more so) is what we do to others. In fact, when James sums up "pure religion and undefiled" he says, "Religion that God our Father accepts as pure and faultless is this: to look after orphans and widows in their distress and to keep oneself from being polluted by the world."[8]

I have known Christians who have tried to impress me with how smart they were or how much they prayed or fasted or prophesied. I knew one minister who started praying twelve hours a day, every day. It didn't do him much good and it did his ministry no good at all.

---

[5] Luke 6.27

[6] 1 Timothy 6.18

[7] Hebrews 13.16

[8] James 1.27

I have also known Christians who didn't try to impress me at all, and who simply lived out their lives quietly doing good wherever they could. They were the happy ones.

Before leaving the plant of good works, I need to warn you about a weed that looks almost just like good works but is actually deadly in your garden. The Thirty-nine Articles of the Anglican Church calls this weed "works of supererogation" - a fancy way of saying works done beforehand in order to impress God and gain his favor. Good works are not done to gain God's favor. They are not performed in order to accomplish our own righteousness. Works, even good ones, done in an attempt to *earn* grace always backfire completely. These kinds of works are not done as a result of faith - they are not done *in* faith - but as some feeble and ineffective attempt to save ourselves (we don't say this, but this is exactly what these works scream). Instead of being something that brings happiness into our lives, they actually turn into sin - "everything that does not come from faith is sin"[9] - they are weeds, not garden plants. Our good works should flow *from* grace and faith, not *to* grace and faith. As we embrace by faith God's salvation as a sheer act of his grace toward us, we *consequently* do good toward others, because "we are God's

---

[9] Romans 14.23

workmanship, created in Christ Jesus to *do good works*, which God prepared in advance for us to do."[10]

If we don't do good works in order to gain God's grace, and if good works are not the basis of our acceptance in him, then why do them? Because they will bring about conditions of happiness. "Turn from evil and do good," the Psalmist wrote, "then you will dwell in the land forever."[11] Is longevity and peace in the land a condition for happiness? It certainly is, and one way to achieve it is to do good to others. James promises us that if we become "a doer who acts", we will "be blessed" in our doing.[12]

Generosity

I once knew a Christian man (he is with Christ now) who made more money than I can imagine and lived very well. He lived, *very* comfortably, on $300,000 a year. When he talked of his trips, and his possessions, and his plans, I always told him that he breathed different air than I did. I didn't have any place in my universe to even consider the life he lived. But what you need to know about him is even though he lived on $300,000 a year, he earned $3,000,000 a year! He lived

---

[10] Ephesians 2.10

[11] Psalm 37.27

[12] James 1.25

on one tenth of his income and sowed the rest of it into various ministries in the Kingdom of God! He was a generous man and God blessed him. He was also a happy man. I also know some people who make next to nothing and are committed to generosity. You don't have to be wealthy to be generous.

Generosity produces happiness because a life of generosity is a "conduit life". If you have ever driven through arid lands where farmers dig ditches or canals to funnel water from a river to their fields, you will have noticed that not only are the fields lush and green, but the canals are lush and green also. The canals live a "conduit life". Their purpose is to deliver life-giving water to the fields, but the water also gives them life. If you cultivate a spirit of generosity, you will be a blessing to others, but you will also enjoy blessings yourself.

> Generosity produces happiness because a life of generosity is a "conduit life."

A life of generosity is about much more than giving money (although it certainly includes giving money). Generosity should be cultivated in *every* area of life, not just the pocketbook. Simply speaking, generosity is giving. It is an act of selflessness as opposed to selfishness. We can be generous with our money, with our time, with our skills and abilities, with our knowledge, with our mercy and forgiveness, and a host of other things. But I will say that if a person isn't generous with his money, then he isn't generous.

Saint Paul had a lot to say about the plant of generosity, and he offers some good guidelines for cultivating this plant in our own garden.

First, you ought to give out of your poverty, not out of your wealth. When Paul thought of the Christians in Macedonia, who dug deep to help out fellow Christians suffering in Jerusalem, he wrote "Out of the most severe trial, their overflowing joy and their extreme poverty welled up in rich generosity."[13]

Some people allow the weed of more to creep into their garden and strangle out generosity. Instead of saying, "I will be happy when I get more", they say, "I will start being generous when I get more." The truth is, they won't. If they're not generous when they have little, they won't be generous when they have more, because more will never be enough. You may think that you don't have enough to be generous. You are wrong. I have seen poverty stricken Christians in poverty stricken countries share what little they had with others. The Christians in Macedonia had themselves endured

---

[13] 2 Corinthians 8.2

"the most severe trial" and were in "extreme poverty," Paul says, but they still found a way to take up an offering for suffering Christians in Jerusalem - they actually went "beyond their ability"[14] in their generosity.

Second, you should give of your own accord. Paul tells us the Macedonians gave "entirely on their own."[15] God isn't holding a gun to your head demanding your wallet or your time or your energy. If you can't give it on your own, he doesn't want it. True generosity is motivated by thanksgiving for the blessings in your life. One of the problems of centralized and socialistic-leaning civil governments is they forcefully take from some people in order to care for other people. Of course, a lot if not most of what they take gets swallowed up in bureaucracy and never reaches those in need, but an even sadder consequence of their methods is they rob people of the very the heart of giving on their own. Studies show that when the government gets out of the way of people's generosity, and stops trying to control it, the direct generosity of the people is always more effective.

---

[14] v. 3

[15] v. 3

Paul *invited* the Macedonians to give, but their giving went beyond his expectation. He didn't beg them to give, instead, they begged Paul to be allowed to give.[16]

What Paul received was a special offering for Christians in need. Some people have mistakenly taken Paul's teaching to be about how the local church is supported. The clear teaching of the Bible (from Genesis all the way through) is that the local ministry is supported by the tithe of the people. This is covenantal giving. It means taking ten percent of what you make and giving it to God through the church. Most churches have a minority that actually tithe, and a great majority who say they can't, but they would like to someday when they make more money. There is that weed again! These folk will eventually make more money, but no church in its right mind should hold its breath waiting for their tithes to start rolling in. But hear this: tithe breaks the back of greed. I have never known a truly generous person who didn't also tithe. If you want to cultivate generosity, begin with tithing. Then give freely in other ways. Tip generously. Buy someone lunch. Give to a neighbor in need. Help a

Tithing is covenantal giving. It breaks the back of greed.

---

[16] v. 4

widow in her distress. Send an offering (regularly, I might suggest) to a missionary. The writing of this book is being made possible, in part, through the generosity of one couple who have lent me their house for a week, and the generosity of another woman who has shared part of her inheritance to get it published! If you are being blessed in the least by reading this book, understand it is the result of the generosity of some Christians you may never meet or know. Now, "pay it forward" and be generous yourself by sowing into the lives of others. (If you aren't being blessed by this book, just keep it to yourself and say nothing to anyone).

Finally, you ought to give cheerfully. Paul told the Corinthians, "Each man should give what he has decided in his heart to give, not reluctantly or under compulsion, for God loves a cheerful giver."[17] The Greek word for cheerful is *hilarion*, and we get our word *hilarious* from it. A few years ago I visited a church in Cabimas, Venezuela, pastored by Bishop Alexander Barosso. When it is time to receive the tithes and offerings at *Catedral Bethabara*, the musicians strike up a happy song and the people come forward with their gifts, joyfully singing and dancing along the way. In that church, the offering isn't *taken*, it is *received*; and it is given with hilarity.

---

[17] 2 Corinthians 9.7

It is impossible to give grudgingly and cheerfully at the same time. "Glorify God generously, and do not stint in the first fruits of your hands. With every gift show a cheerful face, and dedicate your tithe with gladness," the Bible says, "Give to the Most High as he has given, and as generously as your hand has found."[18]

Cultivating a heart of generosity is actually cultivating a heart that reflects God's own heart (he loved the world so much that he gave...[19]). God invites us to a joyous (happy, hilarious) contest of generosity. Some people will never know the sheer delight of this contest because they never give. Here is how it works: God gives to us, and we give to him. Then he gives back to us, even more. Then we give back to him. And so the snowball rolls. But you need to know something before you start the contest. You can't out give God. He wins, every time!

Forgiveness

The final plant I would point out in the Garden of Happiness is forgiveness. Unforgiveness is perhaps the greatest hindrance to true happiness that I know. So many people spend their lives nursing grievances which the perpetrators have long since forgotten, and the unforgiveness does more harm to the offended than to

_____

[18] Ecclesiasticus 35.8ff

[19] John 3.16

those who have offended them. Unforgiveness can not only bind you up spiritually and emotionally, it can even affect you physically and become a doorway to all sorts of disorders and maladies. I once knew a woman who was afflicted with a hardness of soul that kept her from enjoying all that God had in store for her. After a season of counseling and discussion, I led her through a rite of forgiveness toward her mother. When it came time to verbalize her forgiveness, you would have thought I was trying to get her to drink poison! Everything within her struggled against saying the words. Finally she got it out, "I....for...forg....I forg...I forgive my....I forgive my mother." Then something broke inside of her and God began doing a sweet and healing work in her life. Today she is one of the freest and most godly women that I know, but that moment was a turning point for her. She was able to intentionally and with hard work forgive her mother. Today she has a good relationship with her mother, her God and her Christian family. Oftentimes forgiveness does more for the forgiver than for the forgiven.

When we were talking about generosity, I pointed out that cultivating generosity gets us into the "flow" of God, and as we are generous with others we can't help but reap the benefits of generosity in our own lives. The same is true of forgiveness. Cultivating the plant of forgiveness in our Garden of Happiness puts us into the flow of God. God is a forgiving God, and as we become conduits of forgiveness, we reap the benefits ourselves.

The most repeated words in the world are found in the Our Father prayer, prayed by millions of Christians every day, which includes, "Forgive us our trespasses as we forgive those who have trespassed against us."

Forgiveness can be a difficult plant to cultivate, and sometimes it takes hard work. We are usually easy to forgive small or singular offenses, but big or repeated offenses are another matter. One time, Peter, feeling rather spiritual and perhaps a little self-righteous, approached Jesus with the suggestion that forgiving a person up to seven times was mighty good of himself. Jesus responded, "I do not say to you, up to seven times, but up to seventy times seven."[20] Do the math - that's forgiving 490 times - to the same person! Obviously Jesus wasn't meaning that we should keep a checklist and the 491st time we should forego forgiveness. He was saying that, as his followers and as mimickers of God, we should stand in the *flow* of forgiveness - forgive always!

God is a forgiving God, and when we become conduits of forgiveness we reap the benefits ourselves.

---

[20] Matthew 18.21f

In response to Peter's question Jesus told the parable which we have already visited, the Unforgiving Servant.[21] A worker who owed a great debt to his master was completely forgiven of his debt, but turned around and demanded payment from a fellow worker who owed him next to nothing. When the master heard about this unforgiving servant, he called him back in and demanded full remittance, and threw him into debtors' prison until he could repay every penny. Jesus ended the story by saying, "My heavenly father will also do the same to you, if each of you does not forgive his brother from your heart."

You might, properly so, ask a question at this point: "Hey, wait a minute! I thought God's forgiveness was unconditional. I though you said he wasn't counting our sins against us! Now it seems like you (and Jesus) are saying that God's forgiveness is conditioned on our forgiving others." You might think that at first, but this would be a misreading of the text. The point is this: if indeed we have *received* God's forgiveness (it is, by the way, *offered* to all, but not *received* by all), then we will find ourselves standing in the flow of forgiveness. We cannot truly receive God's forgiveness without it splashing onto others around us.

But what about people who have really hurt you? What about people who don't even ask or want your

---

[21] Matthew 18.23-35

forgiveness? What about scoundrels and evil people? Saint Thomas A'Kempis said, "Be assured that if you knew all, you would forgive all." God knows all. And God forgives all.

Let me share with you an important principle about forgiveness: forgiveness precedes reconciliation. The Bible says that "while we were still sinners, Christ died for us...when we were God's enemies, we were reconciled to him through the death of his Son."[22] God's kind of forgiveness doesn't wait for someone to ask for forgiveness. It is given as a foundation that leads to reconciliation. The picture here is not of a defeated foe seeking terms of treaty and surrender. The picture is of a magnanimous king winning the battle through forgiving the enemy before the enemy entreats. Don't wait until you are asked. Forgive from your heart and it will pave the way for reconciliation. Reconciliation is an after product of forgiveness.

Sometimes Christians need to forgive people they will never meet again in this life. What a sad situation to see a person bound up with unforgiveness toward someone who has either died, or become so removed from a person's life that they will never encounter each other again.

---

[22] Romans 5.8ff

A good gardener won't walk around with the weight of unforgiveness keeping him from harvesting happiness. Robert Muller, the former Assistant Secretary General of the United Nations, said, "To forgive is the highest, most beautiful form of love. In return you will receive untold peace and happiness."

Chapter Eight

Leaves

She said son lift up your eyes
To him in the skies
And you'll grow like the mighty oaks.
But you son, created in the image of God
Can become taller than the tallest trees.
-Johnny Cash

Fess Parker owns a winery, and the label on his wine bottles has a tiny coonskin cap. Fess is a native Texan who made it big in Hollywood, first in the role of Davy Crockett in the Disney movie, and then later, carrying the coonskin cap into his next role as Daniel Boone in the television series. As a child, *Daniel Boone* was my favorite show on the tube. In retrospect, it was not only the adventures that I loved, I also love that "Daniel Boone was a man, was a big man." He was "the rippingest, roaringest, fightingest man the frontier ever knew." "What a boon, what a *doer*, what a *dream-comer-truer* was he!" The show portrayed a man who not only dreamed, he *did* what he dreamed. He *worked* his garden, so to speak, and his garden was the wild and woolly outdoors of frontier Kentucky. But my favorite character was Mingo, his Cherokee Indian sidekick (played by Ed Ames). One of Mingo's skills was that of a healer, and it seems that anytime someone was wounded, he would trounce off into the woods picking leaves, and come back with a poultice that would bring healing.

The Trees in the New Jerusalem

The story of human history begins and ends in a garden. It begins with God putting humanity (for all humanity was summed up in the person of Adam) in a garden to work it, care for it and keep it. It ends with a garden in the middle of the City of God, the New Jerusalem: "Then the angel showed me the river of the water of life, bright as crystal, flowing from the throne of God and of the Lamb through the middle of the street of the city; also, on either side of the river, the tree of life with its twelve kinds of fruit, yielding its fruit each month. The leaves of the tree were for the healing of the nations."[1]

Maybe Mingo was onto something. John the Revelator saw the same thing that Ezekiel saw: "And on the banks, on both sides of the river, there will grow all kinds of trees for food. Their leaves will not wither, nor their fruit fail, but they will bear fresh fruit every month, because the water for them flows from the

---

[1] Revelation 22.1f

134

sanctuary. Their fruit will be for food, and their leaves for healing."[2]

Some people think this is a picture of heaven. It isn't. Some people think this is a picture of life after the Second Coming of Christ and the Resurrection of the Dead. It isn't. Much harm has been done through a misreading of the book of Revelation (but *that* is for another book!). What the Revelation is describing here is not a futuristic city that will come in the sweet by and by. It is describing the Church of God. It is describing, in poetic language, what you and I are a part of!

> *Some people think the New Jerusalem that John saw was heaven. It wasn't. He was describing the Church.*

John's first mention of this heavenly city isn't in the last part of Revelation, it is in the first part. He writes to the church in Philadelphia (Asia Minor, not Pennsylvania, although it applies to the church in Pennsylvania as well!), "Him who overcomes I will make a pillar in the temple of my God. Never again will

---

[2] Ezekiel 47.12

he leave it. I will write on him the name of my God, and the name of *the city of my God, the new Jerusalem, which is coming down out of heaven from my God*; and I will also write on him my new name."[3]

Can we take time for a little Bible study? Philadelphia was a city prone to earthquakes (think San Francisco), and every time a quake came, the people ran out of their buildings into open spaces seeking some kind of protection from falling debris. Life was always lived on the edge. They never knew when a quake would hit. They didn't have the peace of laying down, *knowing* that they would be safe through the night. God promised that he would make them pillars - unmoving, steadfast - in his very Temple. However, you must remember, the Temple in Jerusalem was no longer the Temple of God. The religious leaders who ran the Temple had rejected Jesus as the Christ, the Messiah.

Instead, the early church understood that *it* was now the Temple of God. "You also, like living stones, are being built into a spiritual house to be a holy priesthood," Peter wrote.[4] Paul said, "Don't you know that you yourselves are God's temple, and that God's Spirit lives in you?"[5] He also wrote, "For we are the

---

[3] Revelation 3.12

[4] 1 Peter 2.5

[5] 1 Corinthians 3.16

temple of the living God."[6] Later in Revelation, John tells us that when he saw the New Creation he looked for a Temple in it and didn't find one, "because the Lord God Almighty and the Lamb are its temple."[7] The Lamb, Christ, is the Temple, and we are "in Christ" (to use one of Paul's favorite phrases[8]). John isn't describing heaven. He is describing the Church, which we have read, "is coming down out of heaven from my God." This is not written in the future tense, but in the perfect. The heavenly city, it might be translated, "is *even now and always in the process of coming down* out of heaven from my God."

The promise to the Philadelphians (the city whose name, by the way, means "brotherly love") is that Jesus will write upon them three names: the name of his God (Yahweh, Jehovah), his own new name (Christ, "anointed one") and the name of the city itself. What might that name be? Well, we have already seen that its name is "New Jerusalem" or "Heavenly Jerusalem," but there is more - Ezekiel tells us that he too saw a vision of that city - the Church - and that "the name of the city from that time on will be: The Lord Is There."[9]

---

[6] 2 Corinthians 6.16

[7] Revelation 21.22

[8] He uses it, among other places, eleven times in the first chapter of Ephesians alone.

[9] Ezekiel 48.35

Do you see it? God writes upon his new people three names: *Yahweh, the Anointed One, Is There!*

We are already in the New Jerusalem! Someday it will cover the earth, but we are already members and citizens of that heavenly city. The writer of Hebrews tells us that everything that came before the Church, including the Temple and the Priesthood and the Law and Jerusalem, were only types and shadows, but that we have come to the real thing: "But you have come to Mount Zion, to *the heavenly Jerusalem, the city of the living God*...to *the church of the firstborn*, whose names are written in heaven..."[10]

In Revelation, John tells us that the New Jerusalem, which is "even now in the process of coming down from heaven," is the Bride of Christ, and "Now the dwelling of God is with men"[11]. Isn't that precisely what Jesus' title, "Immanuel" means? "God is with us." The same John writes in his Gospel, "The Word became flesh and made his dwelling among us."[12]

---

[10] Hebrews 12.22ff

[11] Revelation 21.2f

[12] John 1.14

Healing Leaves

OK. That's our Bible study for the day. All that to say this: when John saw the Heavenly Jerusalem, he wasn't seeing something in the future, he was seeing something in the present - *his* present and *our* present. He was seeing the Church.

And in the middle of the City - in the middle of the Church - there was a river of life flowing from God's throne which had trees along it whose leaves were for the healing of the nations! [13] Think about it - if this were a picture of heaven, the nations wouldn't *need* healing! But in the here and now they certainly do. The nations (literally, "the peoples") need healing in every aspect of life. This is why missionaries go to foreign lands. This is why Christian doctors set up clinics in desolate places. This is why evangelism happens, here and abroad.

> *Nations don't need healing in heaven, they need healing now! And our leaves are for their healing.*

As you cultivate, nurture and care for your Garden of Happiness (*our* Garden of Happiness actually, for we

---

[13] Revelation 22.1ff

are all in this together), not only will you reap the fruit of happiness in your own life, you will also bring healing to others.

The Fruit of Prosperity

The Psalmist wrote that the righteous man is "like a tree planted by streams of water, which yields its fruit in season, and whose leaf does not wither. Whatever he does prospers."[14] *You* are a tree in the city of God. *You* are appointed to have leaves that do not wither, that bring healing to others, and as you are bearing your fruit and leaves, you will find prosperity in every sense of the word.

Part of happiness is to enjoy *things*. The Bible tells us that God "richly provides us with everything for our enjoyment."[15] Prosperity is God's plan for his people. Consider his plan:

> For Jacob: "Go back to your country and your relatives, and I will make you prosper."[16]

---

[14] Psalm 1.3

[15] 1 Timothy 6.17

[16] Genesis 32.9

For Joseph: "The Lord was with Joseph, and he prospered."[17]

For Israel: "Walk in all the way that the LORD your God has commanded you, so that you may live and prosper and prolong your days in the land that you will possess."[18]

For Joshua: "Do not let this Book of the Law depart from your mouth; meditate on it day and night, so that you may be careful to do everything written in it. Then you will be prosperous and successful."[19]

For Solomon: "Walk in his ways, and keep his decrees and commands, his laws and requirements, as written in the Law of Moses, so that you may prosper in all you do and wherever you go."[20]

For Israel in exile: "For I know the plans I have for you," declares the LORD,

---

[17] Genesis 39.2

[18] Deuteronomy 5.33

[19] Joshua 1.8

[20] 1 Kings 2.3

"plans to prosper you and not to harm you, plans to give you hope and a future."[21]

For Daniel: "So Daniel prospered during the reign of Darius and the reign of Cyrus the Persian."[22]

For Christians: "Beloved, I pray that in all respects you may prosper and be in good health, just as your soul prospers."[23]

It is not merely a material prosperity that God desires for us, but it does include the material (remember, God is not a Gnostic, he made the material world and called it "very good"[24]).

In the first garden, man made the mistake of trading a life-giving relationship with God for a death-dealing observation of the Law (which no one has kept or can keep perfectly). He traded the fruit of the Tree of *Life* for the fruit of the Tree of the *Knowledge of Good and Evil*.

---

[21] Jeremiah 29.11

[22] Daniel 6.28

[23] 3 John 1.2

[24] Genesis 1.31

From that moment forward God has been working a plan to draw man back into relationship with himself, back into the Garden of Happiness. He saved righteous Noah through the Ark (which is a picture of the Church). He raised up Abraham to make him a mighty nation from which one would come who would bless all nations. He raised up Moses and Joshua and David and Solomon and the Prophets and John the Baptist and a little virgin girl named Mary to bring forth that promised Seed. In that Seed - Jesus himself - God became one of us. He lived, died, and rose again for us (and, remember, was mistaken on that Resurrection morning, for a *gardener!*[25]), and the whole world was reconciled to God. Then he birthed the Church to carry the blessings of the garden to all "peoples, nations, and men of every language."[26] And he has now raised up you. To continue Adam's appointed task. To cultivate a Garden of Happiness that brings joy to you and life to others.

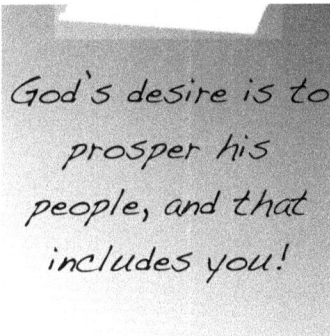

God's desire is to prosper his people, and that includes you!

How does your garden grow?

---

[25] John 20.15

[26] Daniel 7.14, cf. Acts 2.5ff

Epilogue

Understanding the Seasons

For everything,
Turn, turn, turn,
There is a season,
Turn, turn, turn.
- Pete Seeger

There are four seasons in the natural year, and there are also seasons in the Garden of Happiness. Not everything happens at once, and once things do happen, the seasons still cycle and must be lived through. There are seasons for preparing, for planting, for tending and for harvesting.

Christians in liturgical churches have found the rhythm of the seasons in the Church Year. We celebrate Advent, when we anticipate the Coming of the Lord (both his first and final). Christmas is not a single day, but twelve days of celebrating his birth. Epiphany proclaims him as the light to the nations. During Lent we spend forty days uniting ourselves with Christ's earthly ministry and his temptation. Holy Week turns our attention to his passion, death and burial. Easter is fifty days of joyously celebrating his victory over death. Pentecost shouts the good news of the gift of the Holy Spirit. Then there is Ordinary Time, six months of the color green, the color of a garden, a time of growing and maturing and bearing fruit. Then the cycle begins again.

As a final thought, I want to encourage you to be patient in your gardening, and do the right things in the right seasons. Do not become easily unsettled if the seeds you have planted are taking time to bear fruit. Just carefully tend them and weed the garden, and you will eventually reap a harvest of happiness, and you will have plenty enough for yourself and to share with your neighbors - even those in a far off land.

.

About the Author

Kenneth Myers was born in 1959 in Denison, Texas. The son of a pastor/missionary, he married Shirley McSorley in 1977. They have three children and two grandchildren. He is an Anglican bishop and pastors Christ Church Cathedral in Sherman, Texas.

www.kennethmyers.net

www.ingramcontent.com/pod-product-compliance
Lightning Source LLC
Chambersburg PA
CBHW060258050426
42448CB00009B/1680